Microsoft® Access 7 for Windows® 95

Illustrated Brief Edition

Elizabeth Eisner Reding

CTI

A DIVISION OF COURSE TECHNOLOGY
ONE MAIN STREET, CAMBRIDGE MA 02142

an International Thomson Publishing company I(T)P

Albany • Bonn • Boston • Cincinnati • London • Madrid • Melbourne • Mexico City
New York • Paris • San Francisco • Singapore • Tokyo • Toronto • Washington

Microsoft Access 7 for Windows 95 — Illustrated Brief Edition is published by CTI.

Managing Editor:	Marjorie Hunt
Senior Product Manager:	Nicole Jones Pinard
Production Editor:	Catherine D. Griffin
Text Designer:	Leslie Hartwell
Cover Designer:	John Gamache

© 1996 by CTI.
A Division of Course Technology – I(T)P

For more information contact:
Course Technology
One Main Street
Cambridge, MA 02142

International Thomson Publishing Europe
Berkshire House 168-173
High Holborn
London WCIV 7AA
England

Thomas Nelson Australia
102 Dodds Street
South Melbourne, 3205
Victoria, Australia

Nelson Canada
1120 Birchmount Road
Scarborough, Ontario
Canada M1K 5G4

International Thomson Editores
Campos Eliseos 385, Piso 7
Col. Polanco
11560 Mexico D.F. Mexico

International Thomson Publishing GmbH
Königswinterer Strasse 418
53277 Bonn
Germany

International Thomson Publishing Asia
211 Henderson Road
#05-10 Henderson Building
Singapore 0315

International Thomson Publishing Japan
Hirakawacho Kyowa Building, 3F
2-2-1 Hirakawacho
Chiyoda-ku, Tokyo 102
Japan

Trademarks

Course Technology and the open book logo are registered trademarks of Course Technology

I(T)P   The ITP logo is a trademark under license.

Some of the product names in this book have been used for identification purposes only and may be trademarks or registered trademarks of their respective manufacturers and sellers.

Disclaimer

CTI reserves the right to revise this publication and make changes from time to time in its content without notice.

0-7600-3812-0

Printed in the United States of America

10 9 8 7 6 5 4 3 2

From the Illustrated Series

At Course Technology we believe that technology will transform the way that people teach and learn. We are very excited about bringing you, instructors and students, the most practical and affordable technology-related products available.

The Development Process

Our development process is unparalleled in the educational publishing industry. Every product we create goes through an exacting process of design, development, review, and testing.

Reviewers give us direction and insight that shape our manuscripts and bring them up to the latest standards. Every manuscript is quality tested. Students whose backgrounds match the intended audience work through every keystroke, carefully checking for clarity and pointing out errors in logic and sequence. Together with our own technical reviewers, these testers help us ensure that everything that carries our name is as error-free and easy to use as possible.

The Products

We show both *how* and *why* technology is critical to solving problems in the classroom and in whatever field you choose to teach or pursue. Our time-tested, step-by-step instructions provide unparalleled clarity. Examples and applications are chosen and crafted to motivate students.

The Illustrated Series Team

The Illustrated Series is committed to providing you with the most visual introduction to microcomputer applications. No other series of books will get you up to speed faster in today's changing software environment. This book will suit your needs because it was delivered quickly, efficiently, and affordably. In every aspect of business, we rely on a commitment to quality and the use of technology. Each member of the Illustrated Team contributes to this process. The names of all our team members are listed below.

Cynthia Anderson	Steven Johnson
Chia-Ling Barker	Nancy Ludlow
Donald Barker	Tara O'Keefe
Laura Bergs	Harry Phillips
David Beskeen	Nicole Jones Pinard
Ann Marie Buconjic	Katherine Pinard
Rachel Bunin	Kevin Proot
Joan Carey	Elizabeth Eisner Reding
Patrick Carey	Neil Salkind
Sheralyn Carroll	Gregory Schultz
Pam Conrad	Ann Shaffer
Mary Therese Cozzola	Roger Skilling
Carol Cram	Patty Stephan
Kim Crowley	Dan Swanson
Linda Ericksen	Marie Swanson
Lisa Friedrichsen	Jennifer Thompson
Michael Halvorson	Mark Vodnik
Meta Hirschl	Jan Weingarten
Jane Hosie-Bounar	Christie Williams
Marjorie Hunt	Janet Wilson

Preface

Welcome to *Microsoft Access 7 for Windows 95 — Illustrated Brief Edition*. This highly visual book offers new users a hands-on introduction to Microsoft Access 7 and also serves as an excellent reference for future use. It assumes that students have learned basic Windows 95 skills and file management from *Microsoft Windows 95 — Illustrated Brief Edition* or from an equivalent book.

Organization and Coverage

Microsoft Access 7 for Windows 95 — Illustrated Brief Edition contains four units that cover basic Access skills. In these units students learn how to design, create, edit, and analyze Access databases.

Approach

Microsoft Access 7 for Windows 95 — Illustrated Brief Edition provides new users of Access with a highly visual and interactive learning experience. This hands-on approach makes it ideal for both self-paced or instructor-led classes.

Lessons: Information Displays

The basic lesson format of this text is the "information display," a two-page lesson that is sharply focused on a specific task. This sharp focus and the precise beginning and end of a lesson make it easy for students to study specific material. Modular lessons are less overwhelming for students, and they provide instructors with more flexibility in planning classes and assigning specific work. The units are modular as well and can be presented in any order.

Each lesson, or "information display," contains the following elements:

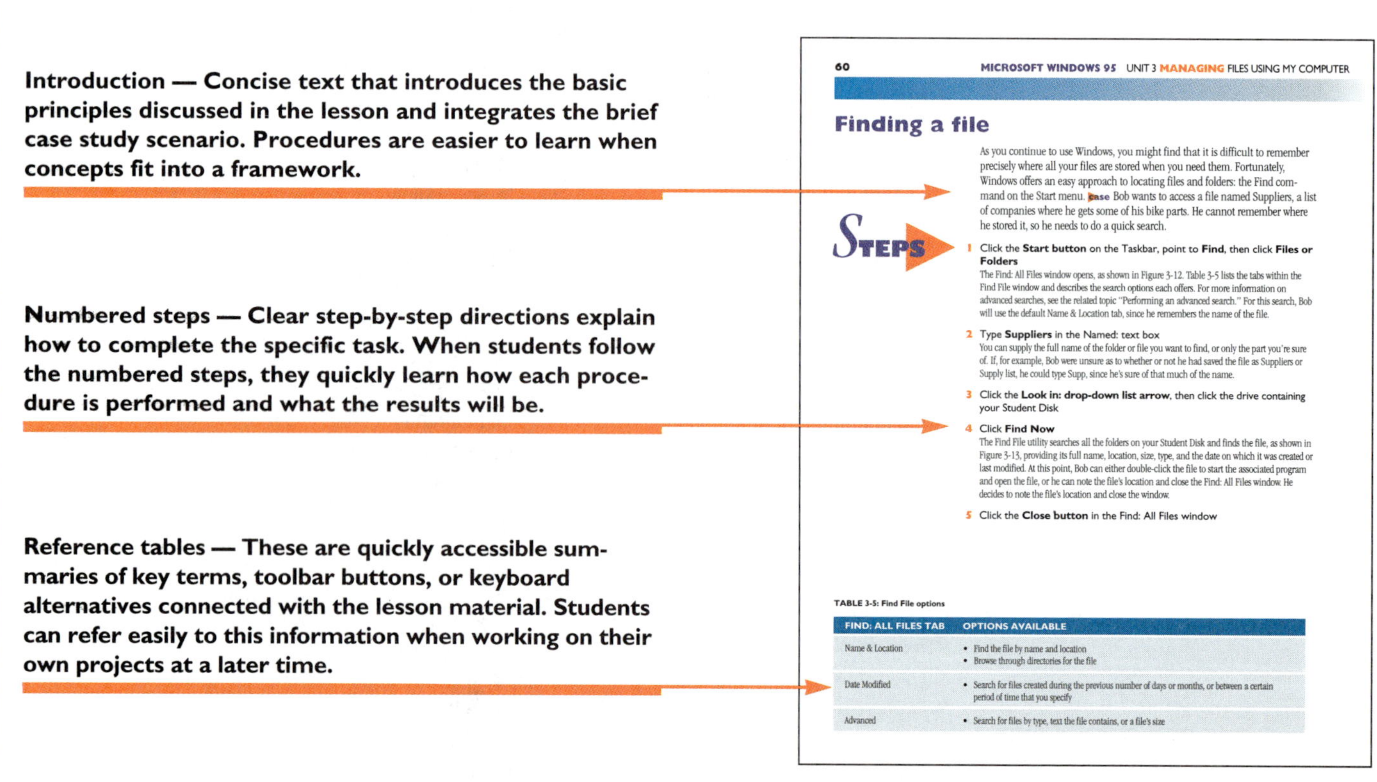

Introduction — Concise text that introduces the basic principles discussed in the lesson and integrates the brief case study scenario. Procedures are easier to learn when concepts fit into a framework.

Numbered steps — Clear step-by-step directions explain how to complete the specific task. When students follow the numbered steps, they quickly learn how each procedure is performed and what the results will be.

Reference tables — These are quickly accessible summaries of key terms, toolbar buttons, or keyboard alternatives connected with the lesson material. Students can refer easily to this information when working on their own projects at a later time.

Other Features

The two-page lesson format featured in this book provides the new user with a powerful learning experience. Additionally, this book contains the following features:

- "Read This Before You Begin Microsoft Access 7" page — This page provides essential information that both students and instructors need to know before they begin working through the units.

- Real-World Case — The case used throughout the textbook is designed to be "real world" in nature and representative of the kinds of activities that students will encounter when working with Access 7. The process of solving the problem will be more meaningful to students. A case icon identifies where the case starts in each lesson.

- End-of-Unit Material — Each unit concludes with a Task Reference that summarizes the various methods used to execute each of the skills covered in the unit. The Task Reference is followed by a meaningful Concepts Review that tests students' understanding of what they learned in the unit. The Concepts Review is followed by a Skills Review, which provides students with additional hands-on practice of the skills they learned in the unit. The Skills Review is followed by Independent Challenges, which pose case problems for students to solve. The Independent Challenges allow students to learn by exploring, and develop critical thinking skills. The Visual Workshop that follows the Independent Challenges in Units 2–4 also helps students to develop critical thinking skills. Students are shown a completed database and are asked to recreate it from scratch.

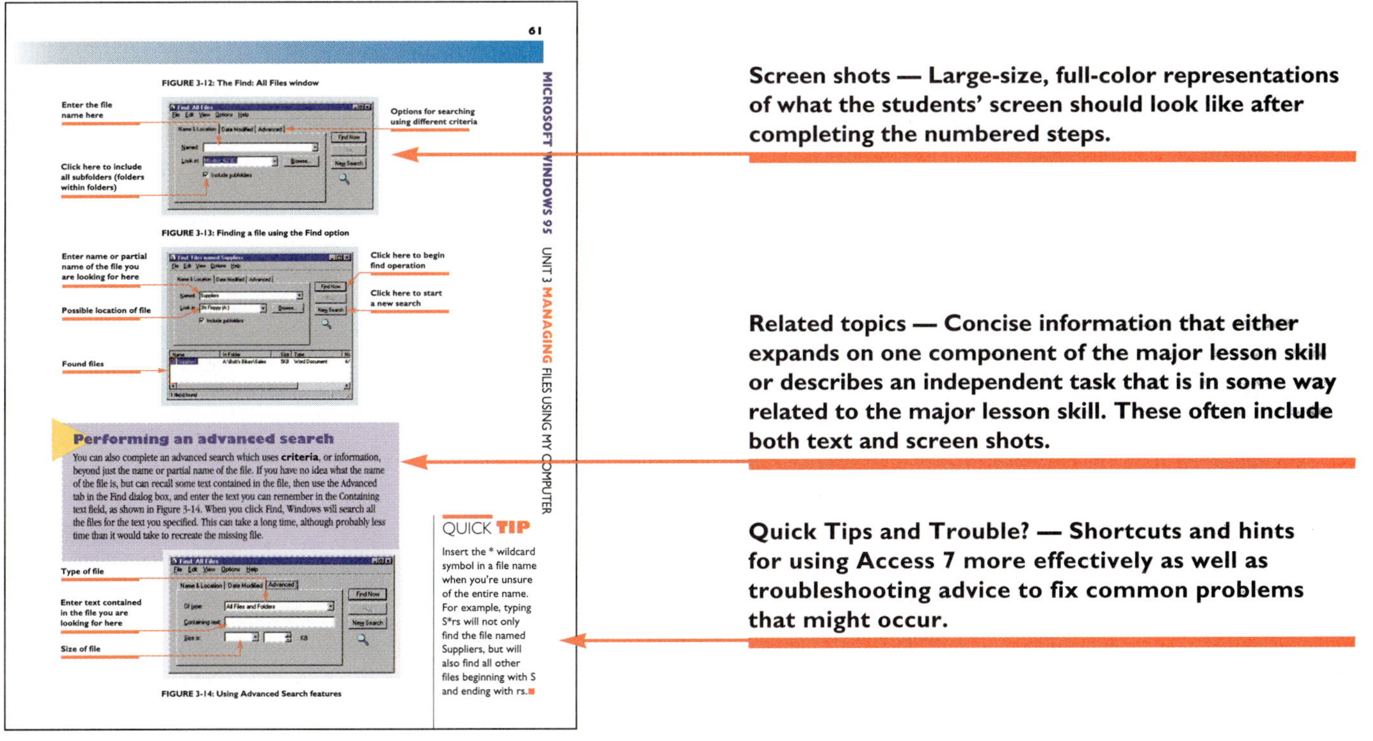

Screen shots — Large-size, full-color representations of what the students' screen should look like after completing the numbered steps.

Related topics — Concise information that either expands on one component of the major lesson skill or describes an independent task that is in some way related to the major lesson skill. These often include both text and screen shots.

Quick Tips and Trouble? — Shortcuts and hints for using Access 7 more effectively as well as troubleshooting advice to fix common problems that might occur.

CourseTools

CourseTools are CTI's way of putting the resources and information needed to teach and learn effectively into your hands. With an integrated array of teaching and learning tools that offer you and your students a broad range of technology-based instructional options, we believe that CourseTools represents the highest quality and most cutting-edge resources available to instructors today. Briefly, the CourseTools available with this text are:

CourseHelp

CourseHelp is a student reinforcement tool offering online annotated tutorials that are accessible directly from the Start menu in Windows 95. These on-screen "slide shows" help students understand the most difficult concepts in a specific application. Students are encouraged to view a CourseHelp before completing that lesson. This text includes the following CourseHelp movies:

- Planning a database
- Sorting records
- Filtering records

Adopters of this text are granted the right to post the CourseHelp files on any standalone computer or network.

Student Disk

To use this book students must have a Student Disk. See the inside back cover for more information on the Student Disk. Adopters of this text are granted the right to post the Student Disk on any standalone computer or network.

Course Online Faculty Companion

This new World Wide Web site offers CTI customers a password-protected Faculty Lounge where you can find everything you need to prepare for class. These periodically updated items include lesson plans, graphic files for the figures in the text, additional problems, updates and revisions to the text, links to other Web sites, and access to Student Disk files. This new site is an ongoing project and will continue to evolve throughout the semester.

Course Online Student Companion

Our second Web site is a place where students can access challenging, engaging, and relevant exercises. They can find a graphical glossary of terms found in the text, an archive of meaningful templates, software, hot tips, and Web links to other sites as well as sites for specific titles. Student sites can be found at http://www.vmedia.com/cti/. These new sites are also ongoing projects and will continue to evolve throughout the semester.

Instructor's Resource Kit

This is quality assurance tested and includes:

- Student Disk and CourseHelp disk
- Solutions to all lessons and end-of-unit material
- Disk containing solutions to all lessons and end-of-unit material
- Unit notes which contain teaching tips from the author
- Extra Independent Challenges
- Transparency Masters of key concepts

Course Test Manager

Designed by CTI, this cutting-edge Windows-based testing software helps instructors design and administer tests and pre-tests. This full-featured program also has an online testing component that allows students to take tests at the computer and have their exams automatically graded.

Contents

UNIT 4   Creating Forms and Reports   *AC 67*

TABLES

Microsoft® Access 7 for Windows® 95

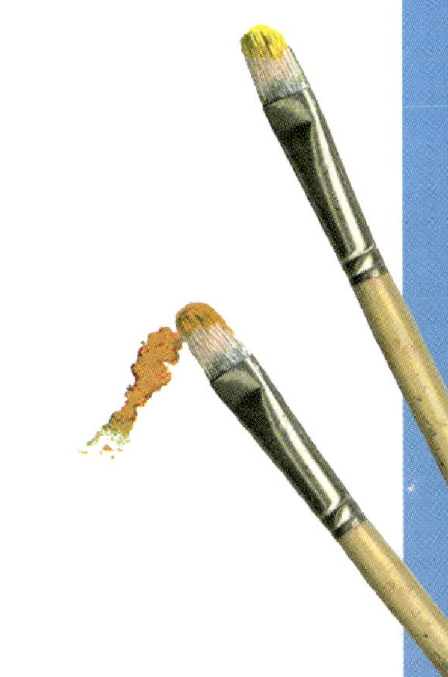

Read This Before You Begin
Microsoft Access 7

To the Student

To complete the step-by-step lessons, Skills Reviews, and Independent Challenges in this book, you must have a Student Disk. See the inside back cover for more information on the Student Disk. See your instructor or technical support person for further information.

Whenever you see this icon next to a topic, you know that a slideshow movie — called a CourseHelp — is available on that topic. To start a CourseHelp, click the Start button on the taskbar, point to Programs, point to CourseHelp, then click Access 7 Illustrated. Then, from the CourseHelp opening screen, click the topic that relates to the lesson.

Additional materials designed especially for you are available on the World Wide Web. Go to http://www.vmedia.com/cti/.

Using Your Own Computer

If you are going to work through this book using your own computer, you need a computer system running Microsoft Access 7 for Windows 95, CourseHelp installed on your computer, and a Student Disk. *You will not be able to complete the step-by-step lessons in this book using your own computer until you have your own Student Disk.* See your instructor for more information on the CourseHelp disk.

To the Instructor

As an adopter of this text, you will receive the CourseHelp disk and the Student Disk. The CourseHelp disk contains a README.DOC file with detailed instructions for installing CourseHelp on a stand-alone machine or on a network. Once installed, students can access CourseHelp movies by clicking the Start button, pointing to Programs, pointing to CourseHelp, and then clicking Access 7 Illustrated Brief.

The Student Disk contains all the files that students need to complete the step-by-step lessons, Skills Reviews, and Independent Challenges in this book. See the README.DOC file for more information. Your students must have the Student Disk and CourseHelp installed on their computers. See the inside back cover for more information on the Student Disk. You are free to post all these files to a network or stand-alone workstations, or simply to provide copies of the disk to your students.

The instructions in this book assume a standard installation of Microsoft Access 7 for Windows 95. It is also assumed that the students know which drive and directory contain the Student Disk. It's important that you provide disk location information before the students start working through the units.

UNIT I

OBJECTIVES

- Define database software
- Start Access 7 for Windows 95
- View the Access window
- Open a database table
- Use dialog boxes, toolbars, and buttons
- Get Help
- Move through a database table
- Close a database and exit Access

Getting Started
WITH MICROSOFT ACCESS 7 FOR WINDOWS 95

Now that you're familiar with Microsoft Windows 95, you're ready to learn how to use Microsoft Access 7 for Windows 95. In this unit, you will learn the basic features of Access, a popular database program, and the various components of a database. You will also learn how to use different elements of the Access window, and how to use the extensive on-line Help system available in Access. **case** Michael Belmont is the Travel Division manager at Nomad Ltd, an outdoor gear and adventure travel company. Recently, Nomad switched to Access from a paper-based system for storing and maintaining customer records. Michael will use Access to maintain customer information for Nomad. ▶

Defining database software

Access is a database program that runs in the Windows environment. A **database** is a collection of data related to a particular topic or purpose (for example, customer data). Information in a database is organized into **fields**, or categories, such as customer name. A group of related fields, such as all information on a particular customer, is called a **record**. A collection of related records is called a **table**. A database, specifically a **relational database**, is a collection of related tables that can share information. Figure 1-1 shows the structure of a database. Traditionally, businesses kept track of customer information using index cards, as illustrated in Figure 1-2. However, an electronic database, like Access, allows you to store, retrieve, and manipulate data more quickly and easily. See Table 1-1 for common ways in which databases are used in business.

With database software Michael can:

Enter data quickly and easily

With Access, Michael can enter information on Nomad's customers faster and more accurately than he could using the paper-based method. He can enter data using screen **forms**, which contain **controls** such as check boxes, list boxes, and option buttons, to facilitate data entry. Figure 1-3 shows customer information in an Access form.

Organize records in different ways

After Michael specifies a sort order, Access automatically keeps records organized, regardless of the order in which they are entered.

Locate specific records quickly

By creating a **query**, a definition of the records he wants to find, Michael can instruct Access to locate the record or records matching his query.

Eliminate duplicate data

Access ensures that each record is unique. Using the paper system, Michael could have duplicate customer records if he forgot that an index card already existed for a particular customer.

Create relationships among tables in a database

Access is a relational database, which allows information within its tables to be shared. This means that Michael needs to enter a customer name only once and it will be referenced in other tables in Nomad's database.

Create reports

Generating professional reports is easy with Access. Michael can produce reports to illustrate different relationships among the data and share these reports with other Nomad employees.

Change the appearance of information

Access provides powerful features for enhancing table data so that information is visually appealing and easy to understand.

FIGURE 1-1: Structure of a database

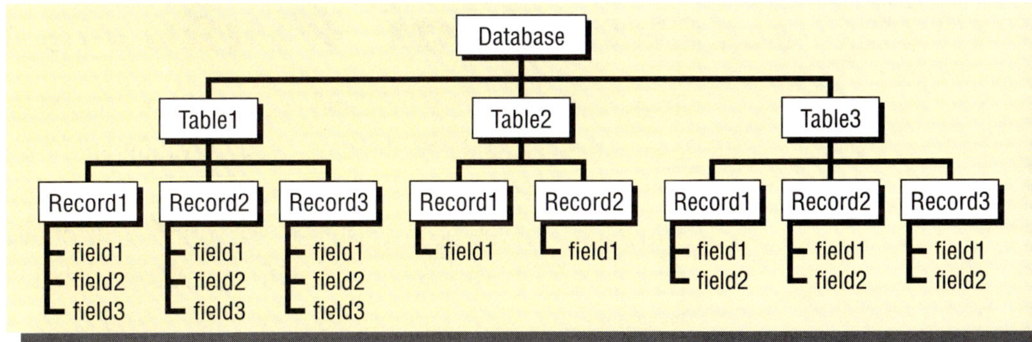

FIGURE 1-2: Customer information on an index card

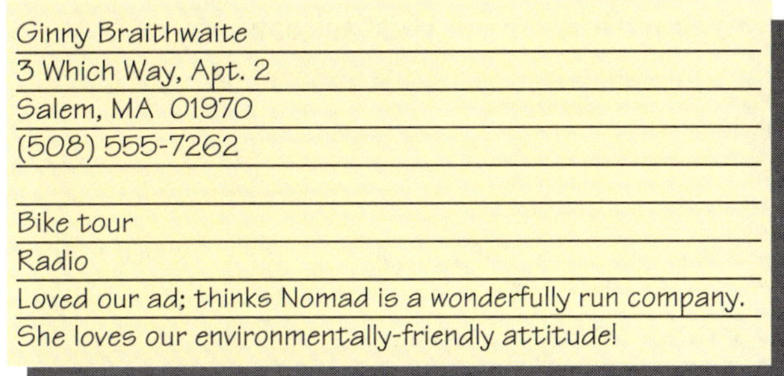

FIGURE 1-3: Customer information in Access form

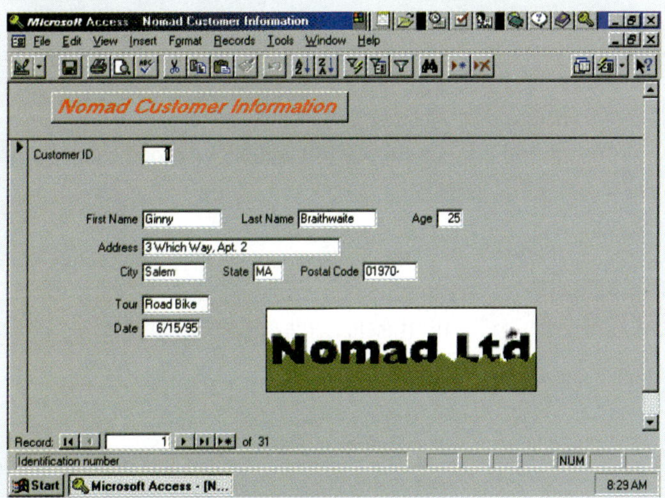

TABLE 1-1: Common business uses for a database

USE	SOLUTION
Storing data	On-screen forms
Maintaining data	Update records
Representing data visually	Charts based on specified data
Manipulating data	Sorting, filtering, and analyzing data
Sharing information with others	Report generation
Locating specific records	Querying tables to find specific records

Starting Access 7 for Windows 95

To start Access, you use the Windows 95 taskbar. Point to Programs on the Start menu, then click Microsoft Access. A slightly different procedure might be required for computers on a network and those that use utility programs to enhance Windows 95. If you need assistance, ask your instructor or technical support person for help. 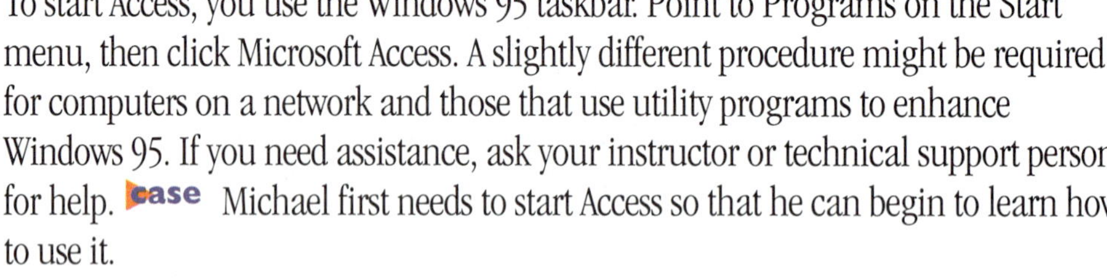 Michael first needs to start Access so that he can begin to learn how to use it.

I Locate the Start button on the taskbar
The Start button is on the left side of the taskbar and is used to start, or **launch**, programs on your computer.

2 Click the **Start button**
Microsoft Access is located in the Programs group—located in the Start menu.

3 Point to **Programs**
All the programs, or applications, found on your computer can be found in this area of the Start menu.

Microsoft Access appears in the Program list as shown in Figure 1-4.

4 Click **Microsoft Access**
Access opens and displays the Access window. A dialog box opens in which you decide if you want to open a new or existing database.

5 Click **Cancel**
The dialog box closes and a blank Access window appears. In the next lesson, you will familiarize yourself with the elements of the Access window.

FIGURE 1-4: Microsoft Access program selected

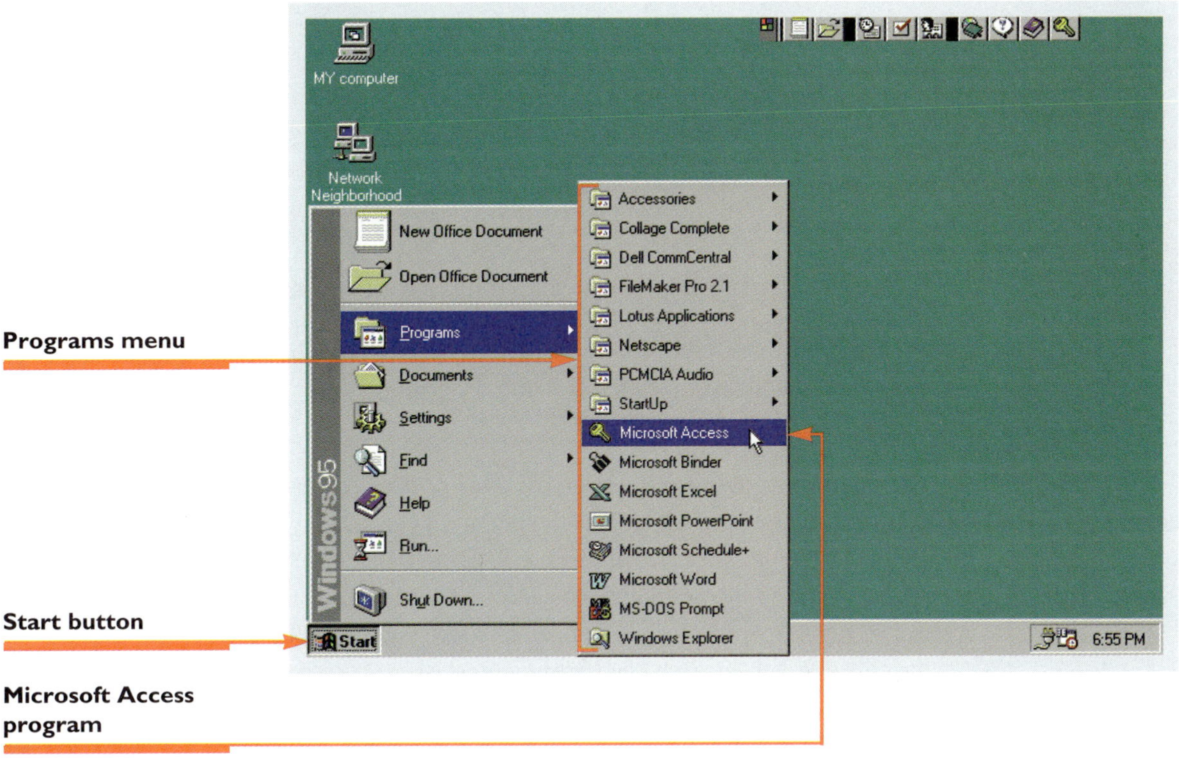

Programs menu

Start button

Microsoft Access program

Viewing the Access window

The Access window contains many elements that help you enter and manipulate the information in your database. Some of these elements, which are described in Table 1-2 and identified in Figure 1-5, are common to all Windows programs. **case** Michael decides to explore the elements of the Access window.

STEPS

1 Click the **Maximize button** if the Access window does not fill the screen

2 Look at each of the elements shown in Figure 1-5
Michael browses through the commands in the File menu.

3 Click **File** on the menu bar
The File menu opens, as shown in Figure 1-6. When a menu is open, the status bar displays a descriptive message about the highlighted command. Some menu commands are **dimmed**, indicating they are unavailable at this time. Some commands include an **ellipsis** (...), which means that when you choose the command Access will display a dialog box in which you must specify the options you want for the command. Other commands contain keyboard shortcuts (on the right side of the menu). These **keyboard shortcuts** are key combinations you can press instead of choosing the command from the menu.

4 Press **[Esc]** twice to close the File menu
Pressing [Esc] once closes the File menu, but File on the menu bar is still highlighted. Pressing [Esc] the second time deselects the menu name. Michael decides to open the File menu using the appropriate key combination. To use shortcut keys, you press and hold [Alt] then press the underlined letter of the menu or option you want to select.

5 Press and hold **[Alt]** then press **[F]**
The File menu opens again.

6 Move the mouse pointer off the menu, then click anywhere in the window (except on the menu) to close the menu without making a selection

TABLE I-2: Elements of the Access window

ELEMENT	DESCRIPTION
Menu bar	Contains menus used in Access
Startup window	Area from which database operations take place
Status bar	Displays messages regarding operations and displays descriptions of toolbar buttons
Title bar	Contains program and filename of active database
Database toolbar	Contains buttons for commonly performed tasks

FIGURE 1-5: Access window

Title bar
Menu bar
Database toolbar
Startup window
Status bar

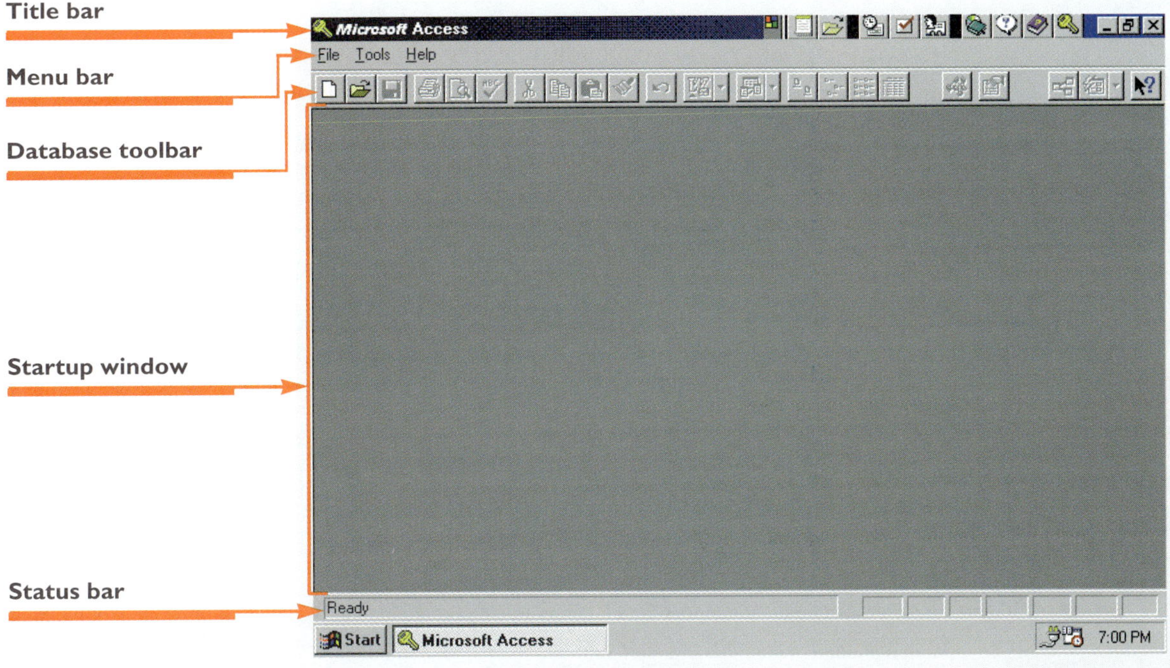

FIGURE 1-6: File menu in startup window

Ellipsis indicates dialog box will open

Dimmed menu command

Keyboard shortcut

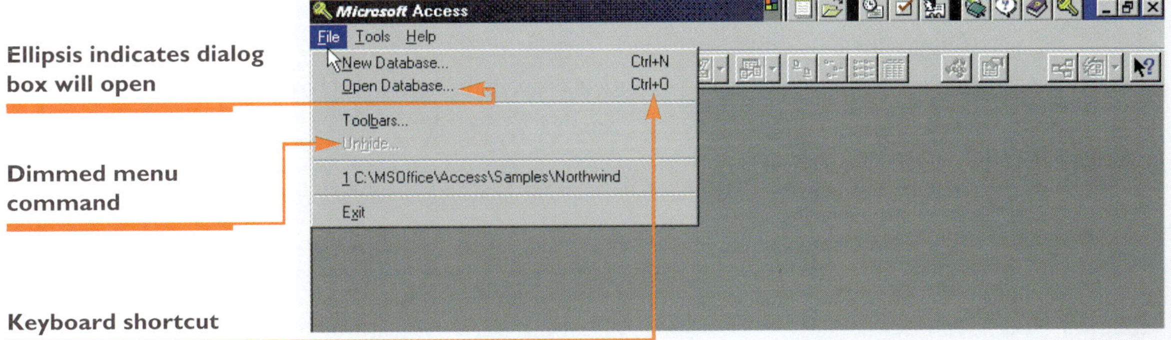

TROUBLE?

All lessons from this point on assume you have Access running. If you need help, refer to the previous lesson, "Starting Access 7 for Windows 95," or ask your technical support person or instructor for assistance.■

Opening a database table

When you start Access, the screen displays the **startup window**, the area from which you carry out all database operations. After you open a database, Access displays the database window. The **database window** provides access to all objects in the database. Table 1-3 describes the objects—such as tables, forms, and reports—that help you use the information in a database. ▶case Michael wants to open a database containing information about Nomad's products to see how it is structured.

Steps

1 Place your Student Disk in drive A

To complete the units in this book, you need a Student Disk. See your instructor for a copy of the Student Disk, if you do not already have one. These lessons assume your Student Disk is in drive A. If you are using a different drive, substitute that drive for drive A in the lessons.

Also, *make sure you have made a copy of your Student Disk*, as instructed on the "Read This Before You Begin Microsoft Access 7" page, before you use your Student Disk.

2 Click the **Open Database button** 📇 on the Database toolbar

Access displays the Open Database dialog box, as shown in Figure 1-7. Your dialog box might look slightly different from the one shown.

3 Click the **Look in list arrow**, then click **3½ Floppy (A:)**

A list of the files on your Student Disk appears in the Look in list box, with the default filename placeholder in the File name text box already selected.

4 In the File name list box, click **Inventory** if it's not already selected

5 Click **Open**

The Database window for the file Inventory opens, as shown in Figure 1-8. The top of the Database window contains the **object buttons** for the Access database objects (which are described in Table 1-3). Each object button appears on its own **tab**, and the Tables tab is currently the front-most tab in the dialog box. The bottom of the window lists the tables in the selected database (in this case, the Inventory database contains only one table, Products). The command buttons at the right side of the window allow you to open an existing table, design your own table, or create a new table. Michael wants to open the Products table, which is already selected.

6 Click **Open**

A window for the Products table opens. The table contains information about 17 Nomad products. The information is organized by fields (columns). Note that the first two columns are both named "Product ID"; however, they contain different information. When this table was created, Access assigned the field Product ID as the Counter field (the first column in the table). The **Counter field** counts the number of records in the table. The second Product ID column contains identification numbers for Nomad's products.

FIGURE I-7: Open dialog box

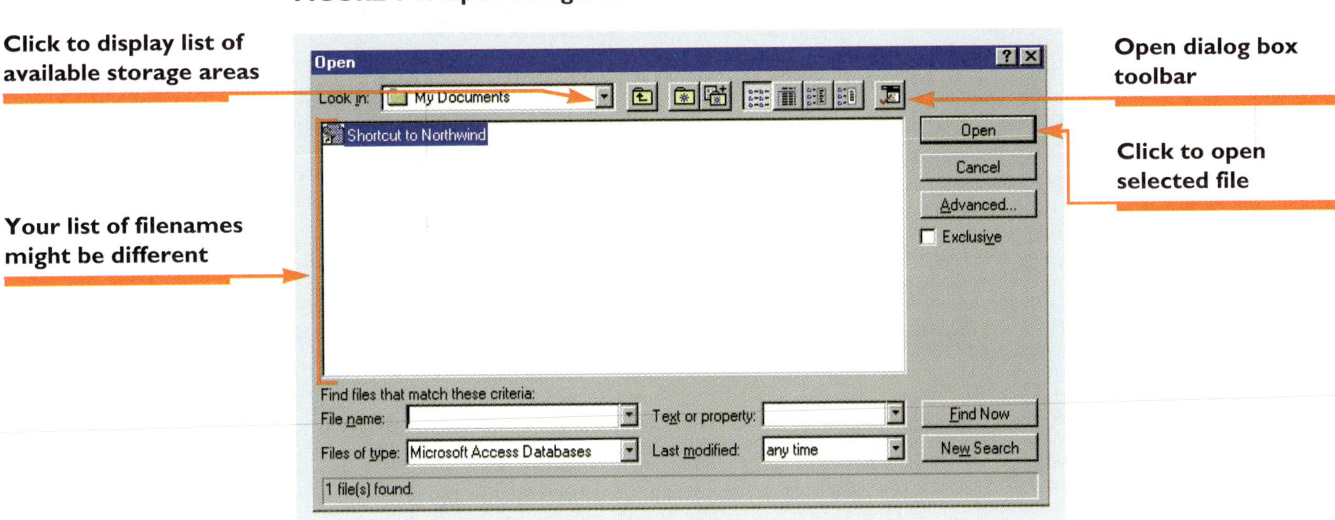

FIGURE I-8: Database window

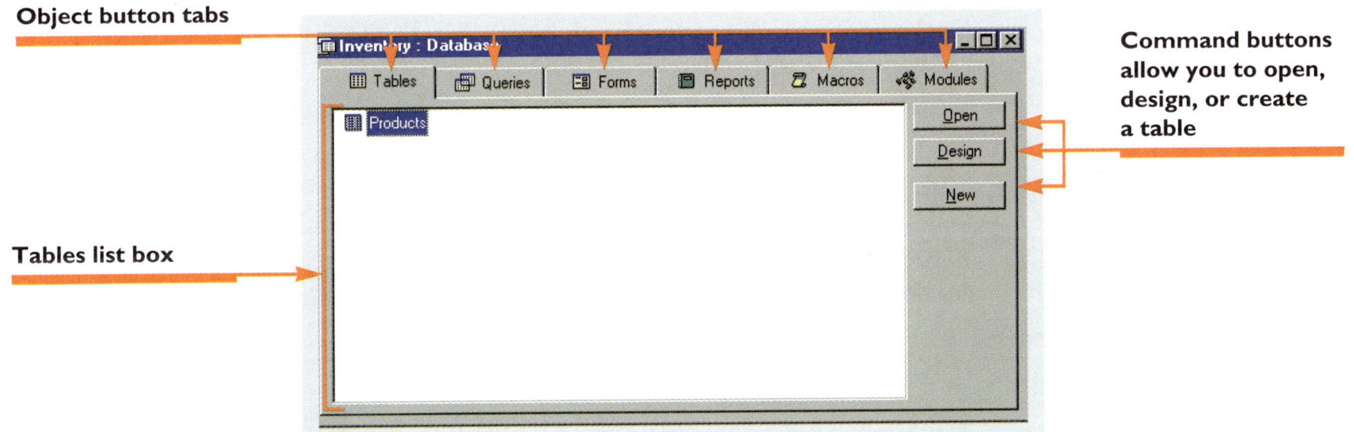

TABLE I-3: Database objects

OBJECT	DESCRIPTION
Table	Stores related data in rows (records) and columns (fields)
Query	Asks a question of data in a table; used to find qualifying records
Form	Displays table data in a layout of fields on the screen
Report	Provides printed information from a table, which can include calculations
Macro	Automates database tasks, which can be reduced to a single command
Module	Automates complex tasks using a built-in programming language

QUICK **TIP**

To open a database file quickly, you can double-click the filename in the File name list box of the Open dialog box. 

Using dialog boxes, toolbars, and buttons

As in many other Microsoft programs, you can choose commands and perform most tasks in Access using either the menus or the toolbars. For more information on choosing commands, see the related topic "Using shortcut keys." Table 1-4 contains a list of commonly used buttons on the Database toolbar. Access contains a variety of toolbars, which appear depending on your current task. ▶**case** Michael wants to explore how to work with dialog boxes and toolbar buttons. He begins by checking to see which toolbars are available in Access.

I Click **View** on the menu bar, then click **Toolbars**
The Toolbars dialog box opens, as shown in Figure 1-9. This dialog box displays all the toolbars available in Access. Toolbars that are currently displayed on the screen are identified with a check mark. Michael wants to display another toolbar.

2 Click the **Table Design check box**
The Table Design toolbar appears. Notice that most of the buttons on the Table Design toolbar are dimmed, indicating that they are not available. You might have to move the Toolbars dialog box down to see the added toolbar. Michael wants to hide the Table Design toolbar and close this dialog box.

3 Click the **Table Design check box** again to hide the Table Design toolbar, then click **Close**
Michael wants to see which buttons are available on the Database toolbar to become familiar with the types of tasks he can perform in Access.

4 Move the mouse pointer over the **Print Preview button** 🔍 on the Database toolbar, *but do not click the mouse button*
When you move the pointer over a button, a ToolTip displays the name of the button, and a description of the button appears in the status bar. See Figure 1-10.

5 Move the mouse pointer over each button on the Database toolbar and read its ToolTip and status bar description

TABLE I-4:
Commonly used buttons on the Database toolbar

BUTTON	NAME	DESCRIPTION
	New Database	Creates a new database
	Open Database	Opens an existing database
	Print	Opens the Print dialog box for the current object
	Print Preview	Opens a Print Preview window for the current object
	Cut	Removes the selected item and places it in the Clipboard
	Copy	Copies the selected area to the Clipboard
	Paste	Pastes the contents of the Clipboard to the selected area
	Spell Check	Checks the spelling of the selected area

FIGURE 1-9: Toolbars dialog box

Check mark indicates
toolbar is displayed

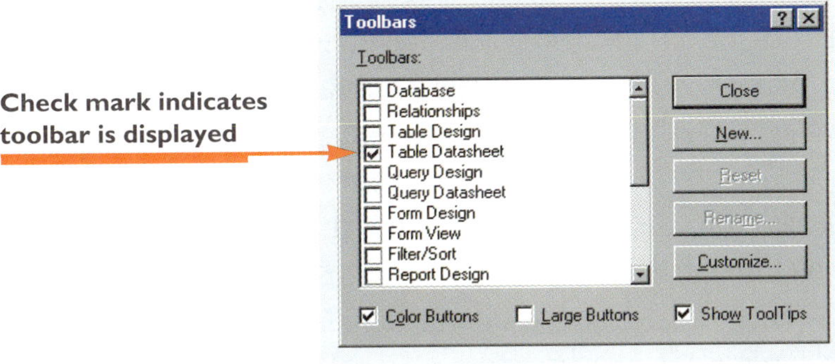

FIGURE 1-10: Print Preview ToolTip

ToolTip

Description of
selected button

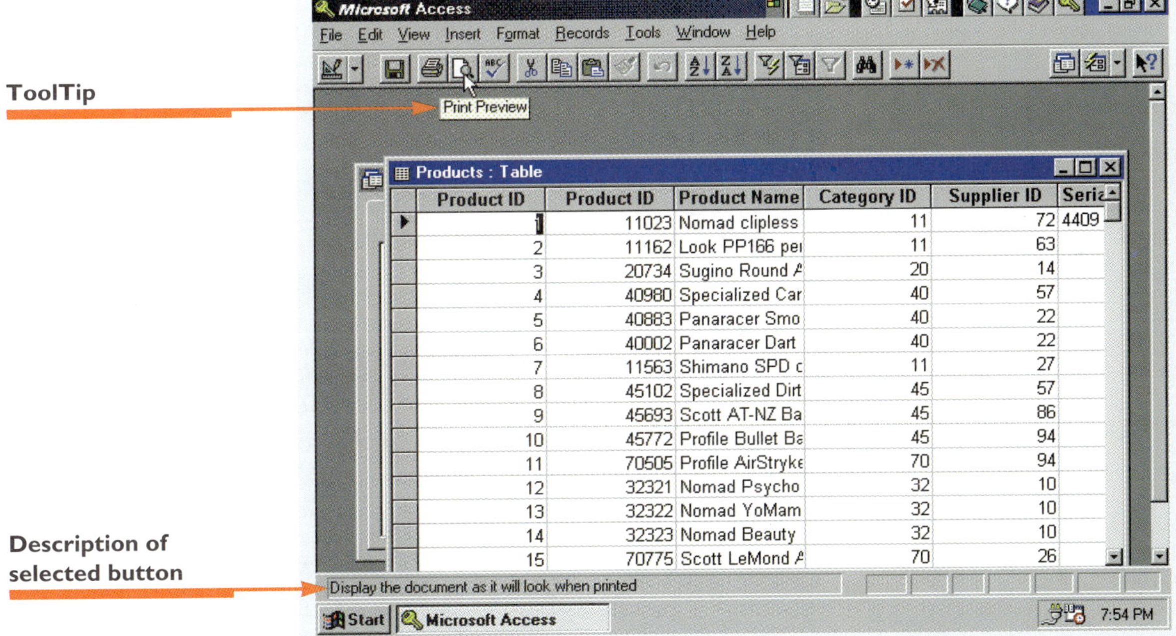

Using shortcut keys

You can use cursor or pointer-movement keys to make choices in a dialog box or menu. To open a menu from the keyboard, press [Alt] and the underlined letter in the name of the menu you want to select. To choose a command from a menu, use [↑] or [↓], then press [Enter] or press the underlined letter of the command you want to select. To open a different menu, use [→] or [←]. To move within a dialog box, press the underlined letter of the command you want to execute.

Getting Help

Access provides an extensive on-line Help system that gives you immediate access to definitions, explanations, and useful tips. Help information is displayed in a separate window, which you can resize and refer to as you work. The easiest way to get Help is to press [F1] at any time, and Access will display context-sensitive Help information for the task you are currently performing. The Help windows contain buttons that lead you through different sets of instructions for Access, as described in Table 1-5. **case**   Michael wants to find information on moving through a database table, and he decides to use the Access on-line Help to do so.

1   Click **Help** on the menu bar, then click **Microsoft Access Help Topics**
The Help Topics: Microsoft Access for Windows 95 dialog box opens. You use this dialog box to look up a specific topic or feature. This dialog box contains four tabs which provide different ways of getting help. The Contents tab is similar to a table of contents: it has specific subjects you can look at. The Index and Find tabs are similar in that you type the topics you are interested in. On the Answer Wizard tab, you can enter a question and Help will answer it.

2   Click the **Index tab**
See Figure 1-11. Using the Index tab, you can type a specific topic or feature and view the entries that provide more information.

3   Type **navi** in the text box
As you type each character, the alphabetically arranged topics scroll in the search list below the text box. After you type "i," the entry "navigation" appears in the list below the text box.

4   Click **Datasheet view**, then click **Display**
The Topics Found dialog box, which lists related topics, opens. Michael wants to read the selected topic, "Moving between records using navigation buttons in Datasheet or Form view."

5   Click **Moving between records using navigation buttons in Data-sheet or Form view** in the Topics Found dialog box, then click **Display**
A window opens containing information on moving between records and fields. See Figure 1-12. Depending on the type and size of your monitor, the window might appear differently on your screen. Notice that when the mouse pointer is on a green underlined topic, its shape changes to ☝. You can click a green underlined topic to open a dialog box with more information about that topic.

6   Move the mouse pointer to the green underlined topic **Datasheet** until the pointer changes to ☝, then click
A window containing information on the datasheet opens. After reading the information, Michael closes the window.

7   Press **[Esc]**
Michael decides to exit Help, then he'll move through the Products table to view the information it contains.

8   Click the **Close button** in the Help window
The Help utility closes and you return to the Products table.

FIGURE 1-11: Index tab in Help Topics dialog box

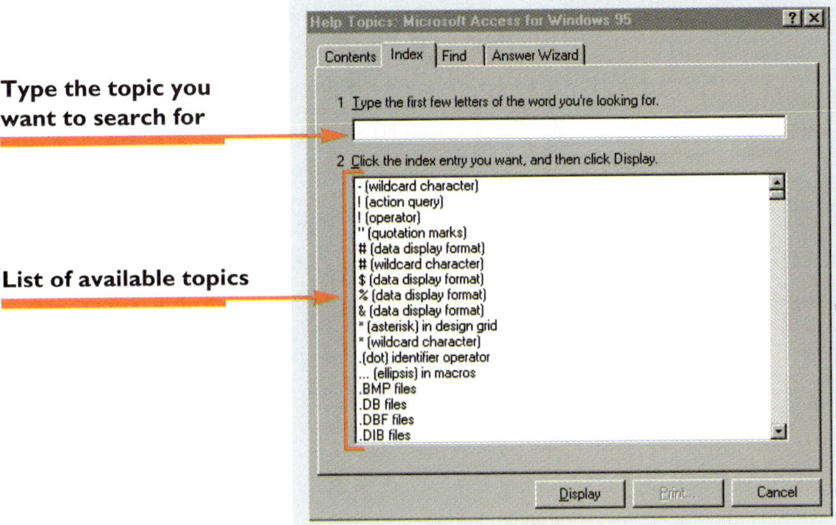

Type the topic you want to search for

List of available topics

FIGURE 1-12: Moving between records Help dialog box

Close button

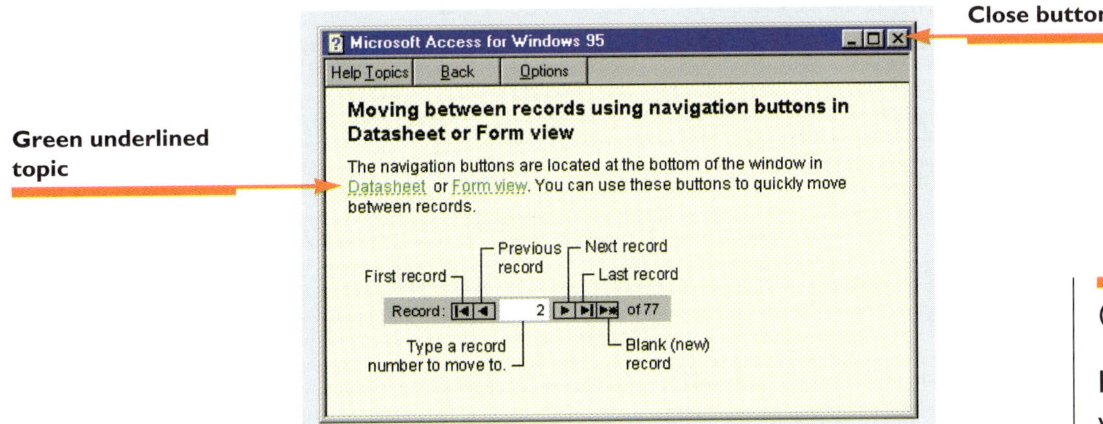

Green underlined topic

TABLE 1-5: Help buttons

BUTTON	DESCRIPTION
Help Topics	Displays the contents of Help
Back	Returns you to the previous topic
Options	Allows you to annotate Help windows, copy the information, print topics, change the font, keep Help on top, change the colors, and display which Help version

QUICK **TIP**

If you need help while you are working on a particular topic, click the Help button on the Database toolbar. The pointer changes to . Place the Help pointer on the object or command for which you want help, then click. Access displays context-sensitive information about the object or command you clicked.

Moving through a database table

When you open a table from the Table tab, Access displays the table in Datasheet View, as indicated in the status bar. **Datasheet View** displays records in a grid format of columns and rows. You can move through a table using the mouse, the arrow keys, or the record navigation buttons at the bottom of the table. Table 1-6 describes the record navigation buttons. You can view fields not currently visible on the screen by using the scroll bars. ▶**case** After reading the Help information on moving through a table, Michael decides to practice moving through the Products table.

1 Press [↓] twice
As you press [↓], the arrow at the far left of the Table window moves down to identify the current record.

2 Click the **row selector button** for record **15**
Record 15 becomes the current record, as shown in Figure 1-13.

3 Click the **first column field** for record **6**
The insertion point moves to 6 in that record. Michael wants to select the Product Name for this record.

4 Press **[Tab]** twice
Panaracer Dart is selected.

5 Click the **Next Record button** ▶
The product name for the next product is selected. Michael wants to move back to the first record in the table.

6 Click the **First Record button** |◀
The product name for the first product in the table is selected. Michael now moves to the last record in the table.

7 Click the **Last Record button** ▶|
The Product Name of the last record is selected. See Figure 1-14.

FIGURE 1-13: Record 15 selected

Row selector buttons

Current record number

Arrow identifies current record

Record navigation buttons

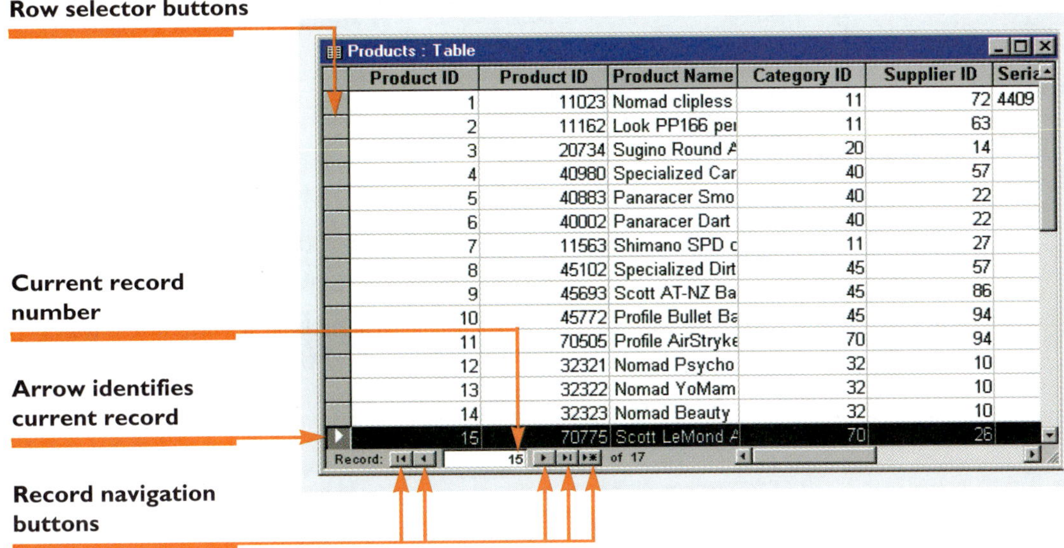

FIGURE 1-14: Product Name for last record selected

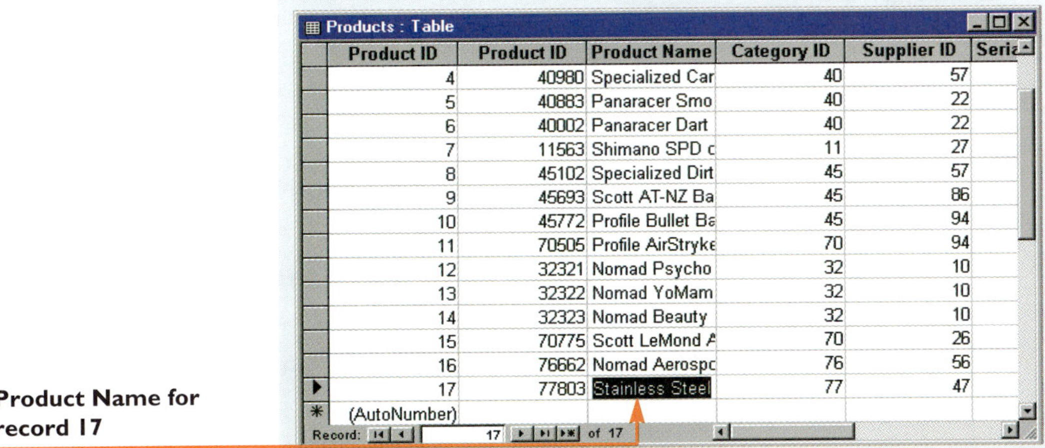

Product Name for record 17

TABLE 1-6: Record navigation buttons

BUTTON	ACTION
I◄	Moves to the first record in the table
◄	Moves to the previous record
►	Moves to the next record
►I	Moves to the last record in the table
►*	Moves to the AutoNumber row to add a new record

TROUBLE?

Don't worry that the product names are truncated, or cut off. You will learn how to fix this in the next unit.

Closing a database and exiting Access

When you have finished working in a database, you need to close the object you were working in, such as a table, and then close the database. Unlike other programs you might be familiar with, you don't have to save a table before you close it; Access updates your changes automatically. To close a table, or a database click Close on the File menu. When you have completed all your work in Access, you need to exit the program by clicking Exit on the File menu. Table 1-7 lists the different ways of exiting Access. **case** Michael has finished exploring Access for now. He needs to close the Products table and the INVENTORY database, then exit Access. Michael begins by closing the Products table.

1 Click **File** on the menu bar, as shown in Figure 1-15, then click **Close**
Now Michael needs to close the Inventory database.

2 Click **File** on the menu bar
The File menu opens and displays the list of commands. Notice that this File menu has different commands from the previous File menu.

3 Click **Close**
You could also double-click the control menu box on the Database window instead of choosing the Close command. Access closes the Database window and displays the startup window. Notice that the menu bar contains only the File, Tools, and Help menus.

4 Click **File** on the menu bar, then click **Exit**
You could also double-click the program control menu box to exit Access. The Access program closes, and you return to the Program Manager.

FIGURE 1-15: Closing a table

File menu

Closes the current table

TABLE 1-7: Ways to exit Access

METHOD	KEY OR COMMAND
Menu	Choose Exit from the File menu
Keyboard	Press [Alt][F4]
Mouse	Double-click the program control menu box

QUICK **TIP**

Make sure you always properly end your Access session by using the steps in this unit. Improper exit procedures can result in corruption of your data files.∎

TASKREFERENCE

TASK	MOUSE/BUTTON	MENU	KEYBOARD
Close a menu	Click anywhere in the window (except in the menu)		Press [Esc] twice
Close a table		Click File, Close	[Alt][F], [C]
Make a choice in a dialog box or menu	Click the desired choice		Press the underlined letter of the command you want to select
Move through a table	◄◄ ◄ ► ►► ►✳		
Open a database		Click File, Open Database, select the file, then click Open	[Ctrl][O]
Open a dialog box		Click menu command followed by an ellipsis (...)	Press keyboard shortcut for a menu command followed by an ellipsis (...)
Open a menu		Click menu name in the menu bar	[Alt]+ underlined letter in menu name
Open a table	Click the table listed in the Tables tab, then click Open		
Search for Help		Click Help, Microsoft Access Help Topics	[F1]
See a ToolTip	Move the mouse over a button		
Start Access 7		Click Start button, point to Programs, click Microsoft Access	
View a toolbar		Click View, Toolbars, toolbar name	

CONCEPTSREVIEW

Label each of the elements of the Access window shown in Figure 1-16.

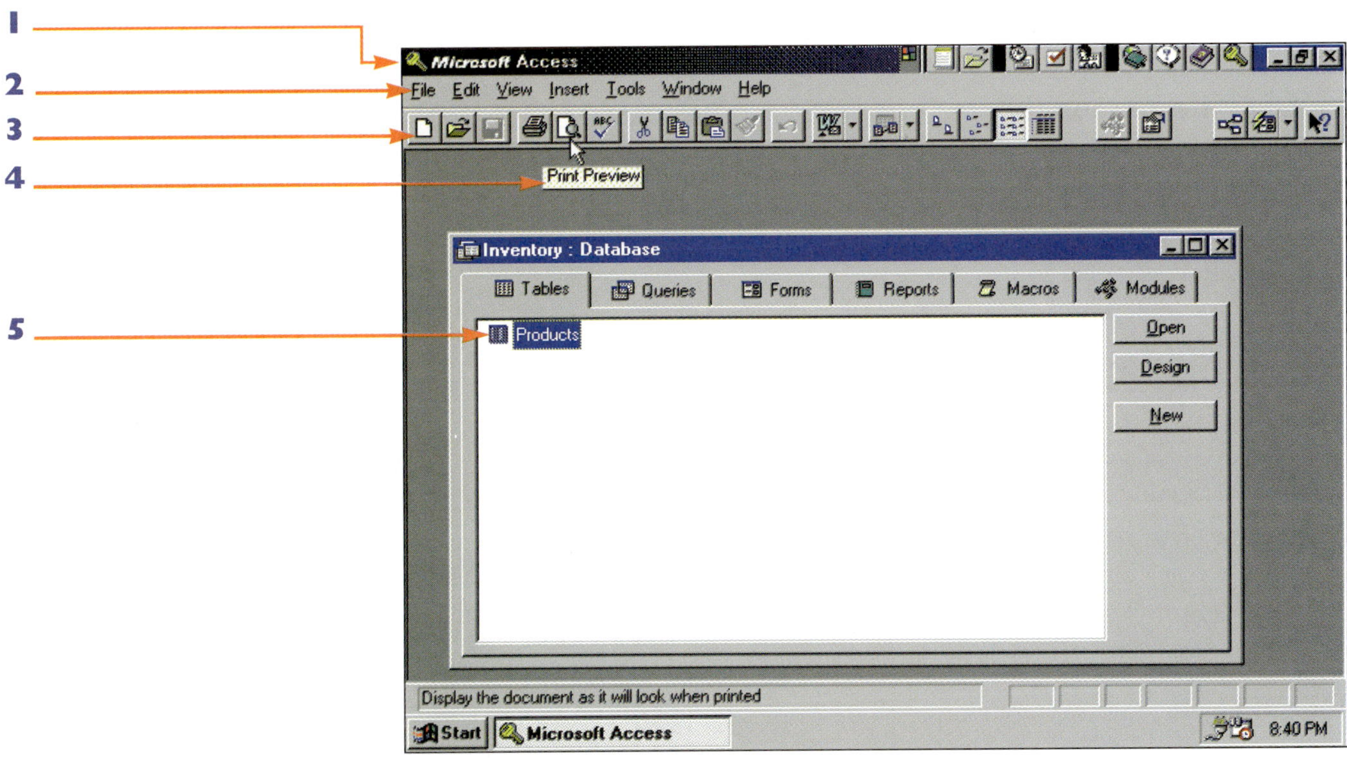

FIGURE 1-16

Match each of the following terms with the statement that describes its function.

6 A collection of data related to a particular topic or purpose

7 Combination of keys resulting in the execution of a command

8 Area that contains all database objects

9 Stores related data in rows and columns

10 The name of a toolbar button

a. Database window

b. Table

c. Database

d. ToolTip

e. Shortcut keys

Select the best answer from the list of choices.

11 An electronic database can perform all of the following tasks, EXCEPT:

a. Displaying information visually

b. Calculating data accurately

c. Planning database objectives

d. Recalculating updated information

12 Which of the following is NOT a database?

a. Customer information

b. Interoffice memo

c. Telephone directory

d. Dictionary

13 Which button opens an existing database?

a. ✂   c. 📋

b. ▢   d. 📂

14 A menu command that is followed by an ellipsis means

a. The command is not currently available

b. Clicking the command will open a dialog box

c. Clicking the command will open a submenu

d. The command has no shortcut key

15 You can get Help in any of the following ways, EXCEPT:

a. Clicking Help on the menu bar

b. Pressing [F1]

c. Clicking the Help button 📐?

d. Minimizing the Database window

SKILLSREVIEW

1 Start Access then identify the parts of the window.

a. Make sure your computer is on and Windows is running.

b. Click the Start button, point to Programs, then click Microsoft Access.

c. Try to identify as many components of the Access window as you can without referring to the unit material.

2 Open a database table.

a. Make sure your Student Disk is in the appropriate disk drive.

b. Click the Open Database button on the Database toolbar.

c. Open the database named US Census Statistics from your Student Disk.

d. Click the object tabs in the Database window to see the contents of each object.

e. Open the Statistical Data table.

3 Use dialog boxes, toolbars, and buttons.

a. Click File on the menu bar, then click Print to display the Print dialog box.

b. Click Properties to see the properties of your printer.

c. Click Cancel in the Properties dialog box, then click Cancel in the Print dialog box.

d. Move the mouse pointer over each toolbar button and view its ToolTip and status bar description.

4 Move through a database table.

a. Press [Tab] to move across record 1.

b. Click the Next Record button to move to record 2.

c. Click the Last Record button to move to record 51.

d. Click the Previous Record button until you have reached record 49.

5 Get Help.

a. Click Help on the menu bar, then click Microsoft Access Help Topics.

b. Click the Index tab, then type "exi" in the text box.

c. Click the topic "Exiting Microsoft Access" in the list of available topics.

d. Click Display.

e. Select the topic "Quit Microsoft Access," then click Display.

f. After reading the information, click the Close button on the Help window to close Help.

6 Close a database and exit Access.

a. Click File on the menu bar, then click Close to close the Statistical Data table.

b. Click File on the menu bar, then click Close to close the US Census Statistics database file.

c. Click File on the menu bar, then click Exit to exit Access.

INDEPENDENT
CHALLENGE I

Ten examples of databases are given below. Using each of these examples, write down one sample record for each database and describe the fields you would expect to find in each.

- Telephone directory
- College course offerings
- Restaurant menu
- Cookbook
- Movie listing
- Encyclopedia
- Shopping catalog
- Corporate inventory
- Party guest list
- Members of the House of Representatives

INDEPENDENT
CHALLENGE 2

Access provides online Help that explains procedures and gives you examples and demos. Help covers such elements as the Database window, the status bar, toolbar buttons, dialog boxes, and Access commands and options. Start Access then explore online Help by clicking Microsoft Access Help Topics on the Help menu. Click the Contents tab, click Visual Introduction to Microsoft Access, click Open, then double-click Visual introduction to Microsoft Access. Explore the first four topics to prepare you for Unit 2.

OBJECTIVES

- ▶ Plan a database
- ▶ Create a database
- ▶ Create a table
- ▶ Modify a table
- ▶ Enter records
- ▶ Edit records
- ▶ Preview and print the datasheet

Creating A DATABASE

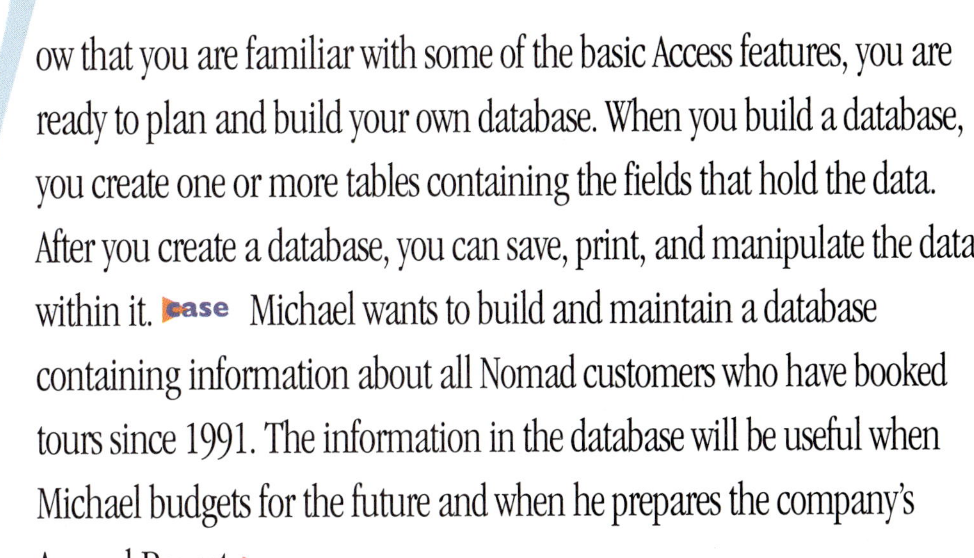

Now that you are familiar with some of the basic Access features, you are ready to plan and build your own database. When you build a database, you create one or more tables containing the fields that hold the data. After you create a database, you can save, print, and manipulate the data within it. **case** Michael wants to build and maintain a database containing information about all Nomad customers who have booked tours since 1991. The information in the database will be useful when Michael budgets for the future and when he prepares the company's Annual Report. ▶

Planning a database

Planning a Database

Before you start entering records in the database, you need to identify the goal of the database and plan how you want data stored in it. Your database might contain more than one table; the planning stage is when you decide how many tables the database will include and what data will be stored in each table. Although you can modify a database at any time, adding a new field after any records have been entered means additional work. It's impossible to plan for all potential uses of a database, but any up-front planning makes the process go more smoothly. Be sure to view the CourseHelp for this lesson before completing the steps. See the related topic "Viewing CourseHelp" for more information. ▶**case** Michael has done some preliminary planning on how the database can be used and uses the following guidelines to plan his database:

1 **Determine the purpose of the database and give it a meaningful name**
Michael needs to store information on customers who have taken a Nomad tour. Michael names the database "Tour Customers," and names the table containing the customer data "Customers."

2 **Determine the results, called output, that you want to see, using the information stored in the database**
Michael needs to sort the information several ways: alphabetically by tour to measure popularity, by tour date to gauge effective scheduling dates, and by postal code for mailings. He will also create specialized lists of customers, such as customers who took a bike tour since 1994.

3 **Collect all the information, called input, that will produce the results you want to see, talking to all the possible database users for additional ideas that might enhance the design**
Michael thinks that the current customer information form, as shown in Figure 2-1, is a good basis for his database table. After talking with other potential users, Michael decides to add an Age field to his table.

4 **Sketch the structure of the table, including each field's data type**
Using all the information on the original customer information form, Michael plans each field, the type of data each field contains (such as whether the field contains text or values to be used in calculations), and a brief description of each field's purpose. Table 2-1 lists common data types. Figure 2-2 is a sketch of the Customers table, including several new fields.

TABLE 2-1: Common data types

DATA TYPE	DESCRIPTION OF CONTENTS
Text	Alphanumeric characters (up to 255 characters per field)
Number	Numeric values that can be used in calculations
Date/Time	Date and time values
Counter	A numeric value that automatically increases
Memo	Alphanumeric characters of unlimited length

FIGURE 2-1: Original customer information form

Nomad Ltd
Customer Information Form
Customer Name: Ginny Braithwaite
                  3 Which Way, Apt. 2
                  Salem, MA 01970

Tour: Road Bike
Date: June 15, 1994

FIGURE 2-2: Plan for Customers table

Fields	Data type	Description
CustomerID	Unique number for each record	Identifies each record
FirstName	Text	Customer's first name (+ optional middle initial)
LastName	Text	Customer's last name
Address	Text	Customer's street address
City	Text	Customer's city
State	Text	Customer's state
PostalCode	Text	Customer's zip code
Tour	Text	Type of tour
Date	Date/Time	Starting date of tour
Age	Number	Customer's age

Viewing CourseHelp

The camera icon indicates there is a CourseHelp available for this lesson. CourseHelps are on-screen slide shows that bring difficult concepts to life. Your instructor received a CourseHelp disk and should have installed it on the machine you are using. To start CourseHelp, click the Start button, point to Programs, point to CourseHelp, then click Microsoft Access Illustrated. In the main CourseHelp window, click the topic that corresponds to this lesson. Because CourseHelp runs in a separate window, you can start and view a movie even if you're in the middle of completing a lesson. Once the movie is finished, you can click the Access program button on the taskbar and continue with the lessons, right where you left off. You can see a list of all the CourseHelps available with this book in the Preface. CourseHelp icons also appear in the table of contents.

Creating a database

After planning the structure of the database, the next step is to create the database file. This file will contain all the objects—such as tables, forms, reports, and queries—that will be used to enter and manipulate the data. When you create a database, you assign it a name. This filename can contain up to 255 characters, consisting of lowercase and uppercase letters, numbers, symbols, as well as spaces and commas. Access automatically adds the file extension .MDB to the filename, but this extension is not visible when you see the file's icon. See the related topic "Filenames and extensions" for more information in filenaming conventions. ▶**case** With his plan complete, Michael is ready to create the Tour Customers database file.

STEPS

1 Start Access then insert your Student Disk in the disk drive
Make sure you have made a copy of your Student Disk, as instructed on the "Read This Before You Begin Microsoft Access 7" page, before you use your Student Disk. The Microsoft Access dialog box opens. See the QuickTip on the next page if Access is already running.

2 Click the Blank database radio button in the Create a New Database Section of the dialog box, then click OK
The File New Database dialog box opens, as shown in Figure 2-3.

3 Type Tour Customers in the File name text box to replace the selected default filename

4 Click the Save in list arrow, then click 3½ Floppy (A:)
These lessons assume that your Student Disk is in drive A. If you are using a different drive or storing your practice files on a network, click the appropriate drive.
Create a new folder where you will save your new Access work files.

5 Click the Create New Folder button 📁, type My Access Files in the Name box, then click OK

6 Double-click the My Access Files folder
The Tour Customers database file will be saved on your Student Disk in the My Access Files folder, as shown in Figure 2-4.

7 Click Create
The Database window opens, displaying the new, empty database, as shown in Figure 2-5.

FIGURE 2-3: File New Database dialog box

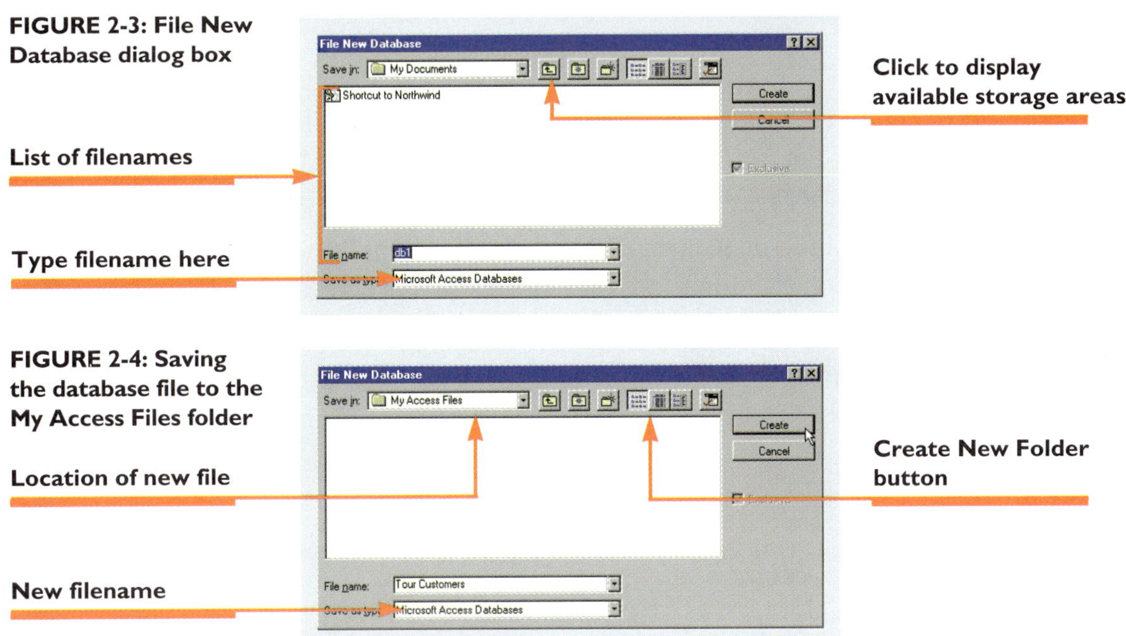

Click to display available storage areas

List of filenames

Type filename here

FIGURE 2-4: Saving the database file to the My Access Files folder

Location of new file

Create New Folder button

New filename

FIGURE 2-5: Empty Tour Customers: Database window

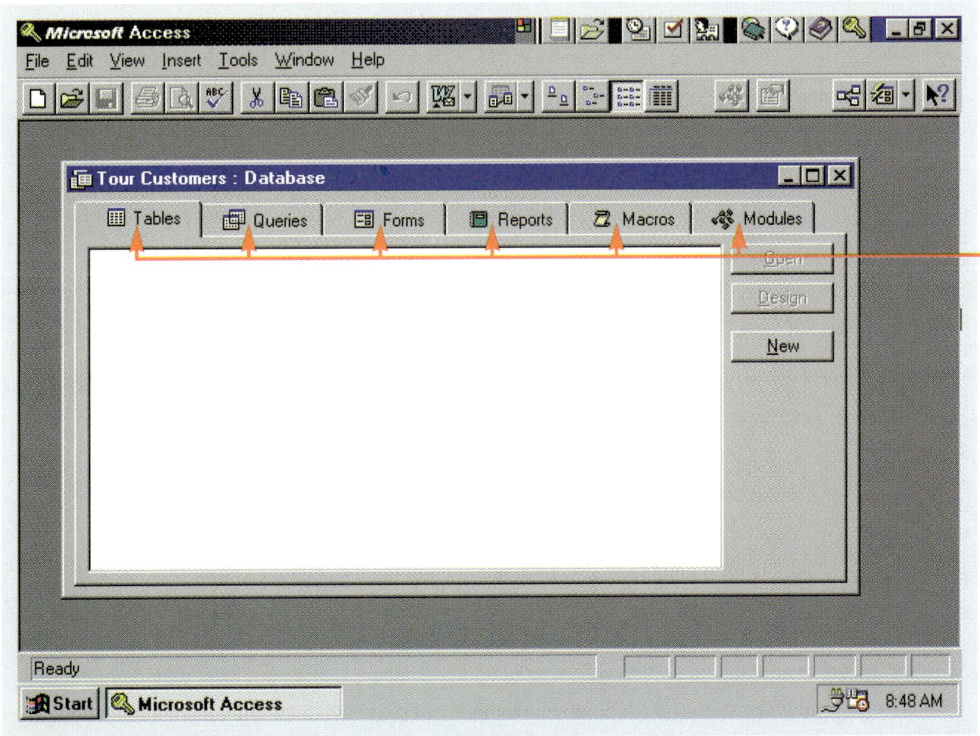

Object tabs

Filenames and extensions

When you save a file, Access automatically adds the extension .mdb to the filename. Unlike previous versions of Access, the extension does not display in the title bar. Windows 95 allows you to have filenames up to 255 characters in length. Filenames can use lowercase or uppercase letters, numbers, symbols, and spaces.

QUICK TIP

If Access is already running, you can click the New Database button on the Database toolbar to create a database.

TROUBLE?

If you need help starting Access, refer to the lesson, "Starting Access 7 for Window 95" in Unit 1.

Creating a table

Now that you've created the database file, you are ready to create the table (or tables) in the database. Creating a table is easy using the Access Table Wizard. The **Table Wizard** guides you through the process of creating a simple table, prompting you to choose the fields and options for your table. For more information on creating a table, see the related topic "Creating a table manually." ▶**case** Using his sketch as a guide, Michael will use the Table Wizard to create his Customers table.

1 In the Tour Customers: Database window, click the **Tables tab**, if necessary, then click **New**
The New dialog box opens. Michael uses the Table Wizard to create the new table.

2 Click **Table Wizard**, then click **OK**
The Table Wizard dialog box opens, as shown in Figure 2-6. The Table Wizard offers 25 business and 20 personal sample tables from which you can choose. Each sample table provides sample fields related to the specific table type. Michael will choose fields from the Customers sample table to include in his Customers table.

3 Make sure the Business radio button is selected, then click **Customers** in the Sample Tables list box
The Sample Fields entries listed relate to customer information. Michael will choose the fields from this list that match his plan.

4 Click **CustomerID** in the Sample Fields list box, then click the **Single Field button** 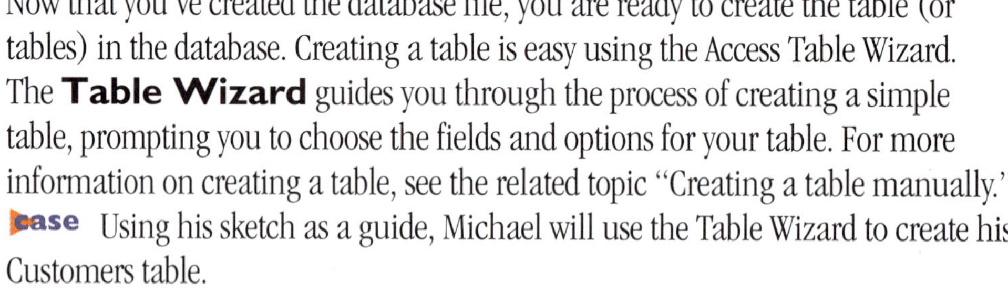
The CustomerID field moves into the Fields in my new table box. Michael proceeds to add all the necessary fields for his table.

5 Repeat Step 4 to enter the following fields in the table: **ContactFirstName**, **Contact LastName**, **BillingAddress**, **City**, **StateOrProvince**, and **PostalCode**
Compare your Table Wizard dialog box to Figure 2-7. Because Michael will only be entering states (not provinces) he decides to rename that field.

6 Click **StateOrProvince** in the Fields in my new table box, click **Rename Field**, then edit the field so that it's named State and click **OK**

7 Click **Next**
The second Table Wizard dialog box opens. Michael intended to name the table "Customers," which Access suggests in this dialog box. He also wants Access to set the **primary key**, a field that qualifies each record as unique. If you do not specify a primary key, Access will create one for you.

8 Make sure the "Yes" radio button is selected, then click **Next**
The third Table Wizard dialog box opens, as shown in Figure 2-8. Michael wants to modify the table's design to include fields specific to his database.

9 Click the **Modify the table design radio button**, then click **Finish**
The table opens in Design view, which allows you to add, delete, or modify the table's structure.

FIGURE 2-6:
First Table Wizard
dialog box

Make sure this is
selected

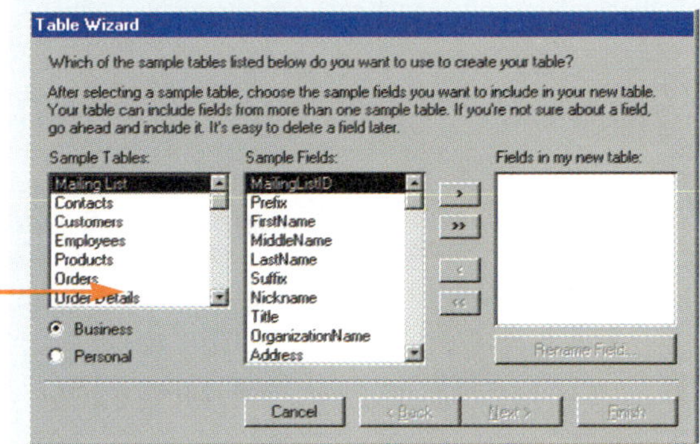

FIGURE 2-7:
Completed Fields in
my new table list

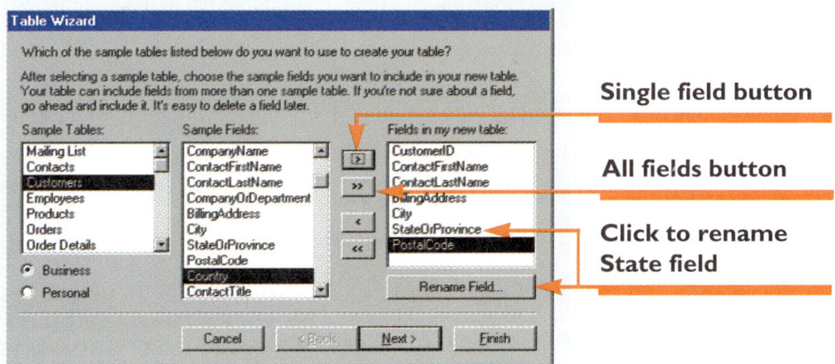

FIGURE 2-8: Third
Table Wizard
dialog box

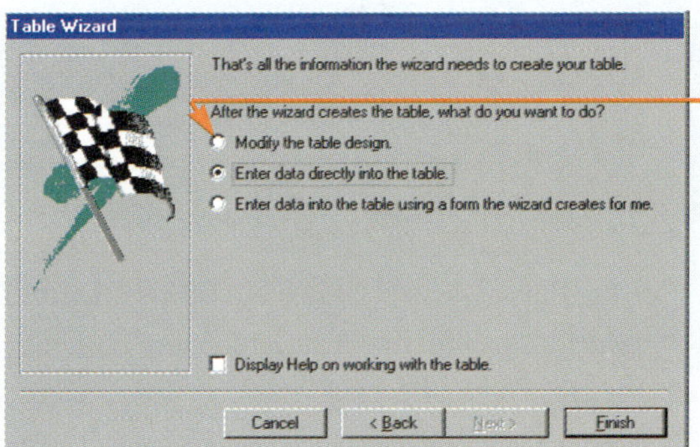

Creating a table manually

You can create a table manually, without using the Table Wizard, by clicking the
New Table button in the New Table dialog box. No sample tables or sample fields
are available; you create any field names you want. Field names can contain up to
64 characters including letters, numbers, spaces, and some special characters. You
might want to create a table manually if your application is unique or your fields
are unusual.

TROUBLE?

If you inadvertently
add the wrong
sample field while
in the first Table
Wizard dialog box,
select the field then
click the Remove
Field button
to return the field
to the Sample Fields
list box.

Modifying a table

After creating a table, you can modify it in **Design view**. Design view allows you to modify the structure of a table by adding and deleting fields, and adding **field descriptions**, which clarify the purpose or function of a field and appear in the status bar when you enter data. You can also define **field properties**, such as the number of decimal places in a number field, in Design view. ►**case**   Using the Table Wizard, Michael was able to add all but three of the fields in his table. Now, in Design view, he'll add the three remaining fields, add field descriptions, and modify certain field properties.

1   **Make sure the Customers table is open in Design view, as shown in Figure 2-9**
If you closed the table at the end of the previous lesson, click the table name in the Database window, then click Design. Notice the row selectors at the left edge of the table. The selectors can contain **indicators**, such as the primary key indicator in Figure 2-9. Michael begins by adding a new field, Tour, in the first available blank row. This field will identify the type of tour taken by each Nomad customer.

2   **Scroll the window until the eighth row is visible, click in the Field Name box in the eighth row (under PostalCode), type Tour, then press [Enter]**
The Data Type field becomes highlighted and displays the word "Text." The Tour field will contain text information, so Michael accepts this suggested data type and enters a description for the field. See Table 2-2 for a description of the available data types.

3   **Press [Enter], type Type of tour, then press [Enter]**
The next field Michael enters is a date field, which will contain the date the tour was taken. A date field has a data type of Date/Time, which Michael specifies by typing the letter "d."

4   **Type Date, press [Enter], type d, press [Enter], type Starting date of tour in the Description column, then press [Enter]**
When you type "d" the Data Type field changes to Date/Time. The last field Michael must enter is the Age field. This field will contain the age of the tour participant. Michael specifies the data type for a number field by typing the letter "n."

5   **Type Age, press [Enter], then type n**
By default, number fields are displayed with two decimal places. Because this is not an appropriate format for a person's age, Michael needs to change the format of the number. To do so he presses [F6] to move to the Field Properties section of the window.

6   **Press [F6] to switch panes to the Field Properties section**
Currently the Decimal Places box displays the option "Auto," which specifies the default two decimal places. Michael needs to change the number of decimal places so that the ages will appear as whole numbers.

7   **Click in the Decimal Places box, click the list arrow, then click 0 to specify whole numbers**
Continue with the next lesson to finish modifying the table.

FIGURE 2-9: Table in Design view

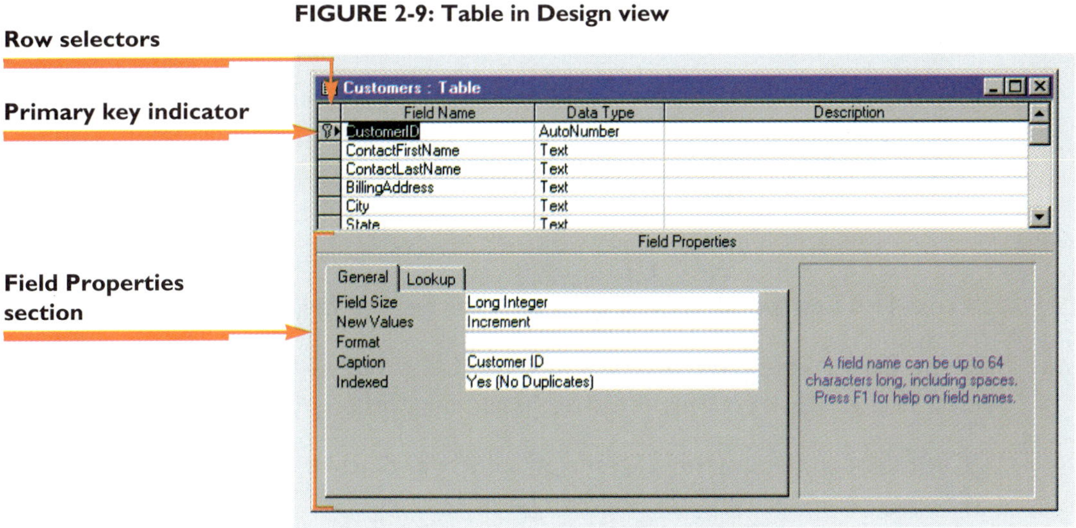

Row selectors

Primary key indicator

Field Properties section

Creating a backup

The information in your database is very important. You should protect your investment of time spent planning the database and entering data in it by creating backup copies of the database file. The database file, which has the extension.MDB, should be copied to a disk or tape on a daily or weekly basis.

TABLE 2-2: Available Data Types

DATA TYPE	DESCRIPTION
Text	Text or a combination of text and numbers that don't require calculations
Memo	Lengthy text or a combination of text and numbers
Number	Numeric data to be used in calculations
Date/Time	Date and time values
Currency	Currency values and numeric data used in calculations
AutoNumber	Unique sequential number that Access assigns to each new record; can't be edited
Yes/No	Fields that can contain only one of two values
OLE object	An object (such as a Word document) that is linked or embedded in an Access table
Lookup Wizard	Creates a field that allows you to choose a value from another table or from a list of values

Modifying a table, continued

Next Michael needs to add a description for each of the fields he entered. For more information on modifying table entries, see the related topic "Editing table entries."

8 Press **[F6]** to switch panes, then click in the Age field Description box

9 Type **Enter the Customer's age at the time of the tour**
Next Michael adds descriptions for each of the remaining fields.

10 Click in each field name's Description box and add a description for the first seven fields using the following entries:

Field Name	Description
CustomerID	Identification number
ContactFirstName	Customer's first name (and optional middle initial)
ContactLastName	Customer's last name
BillingAddress	Customer's street address
City	Customer's city
State	Customer's state
PostalCode	Customer's zip code

The visible fields in your table should look like Figure 2-10. Now that he has entered and modified all the fields in the table, Michael saves the modified table structure.

11 Click the **Save button**

FIGURE 2-10: Table containing field descriptions

Descriptions of fields

Current record indicator

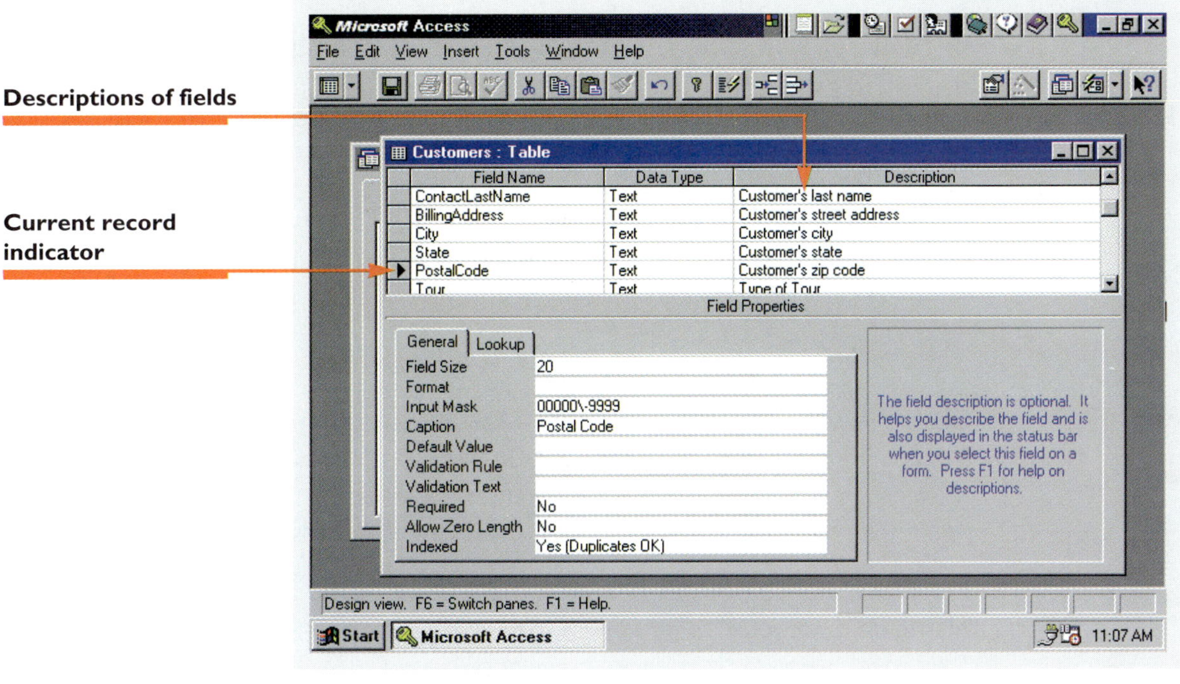

Editing table entries

You can edit any table entry, such as a field name, data type, or description, by selecting the entry then pressing [Delete] or [Backspace] to remove the error. You can modify the field type by selecting the current entry, then clicking the list arrow in the field type box and making another selection. Clicking the Design button on the Database window opens the table in Design view, which allows you to modify the table structure.

QUICK TIP

When entering field information in a column, you can use [↓] to complete the entry and move to the field below. ■

Entering records

After you create the table structure, you enter the data for the table in the **datasheet**, a grid in which each record is contained in a row and field names are listed as column headings. Careful data entry is vital to obtaining accurate reports from the database. If you enter data carelessly, the results of searches for particular information might be incorrect. ►**case**   Michael is now ready to enter the records for the Customers table into the datasheet. First, he will maximize the datasheet window and resize the table columns.

I Click **View** on the menu bar, click **Datasheet**, then click the **Maximize button** in the datasheet window title bar
The window is maximized, and all the fields are the same size, even though the fields do not require the same amount of space. Michael wants to resize the fields.

2 Move the mouse pointer between the Customer ID and Contact First Name field names
The pointer changes to ↔ as shown in Figure 2-11.

3 Double-click the **left mouse button**
The field width for Customer ID adjusts to the width of the field name. You can also adjust the field width by dragging the mouse pointer when it is between the field names. Michael will resize all the fields in the table to the width of the field names.

4 Repeat steps 2 and 3 until all the fields are resized, as shown in Figure 2-12
You might have to scroll to see the last few field names. Now you are ready to enter records. When you enter a record, the word "AutoNumber" appears below the current record. This is the primary key assigned by Access.

5 Click the **Contact First Name field**, type **Ginny**, press **[Enter]**, type **Braithwaite**, press **[Enter]**, type **3 Which Way, Apt. 2**, press **[Enter]**, type **Salem**, press **[Enter]**, type **MA**, press **[Enter]**, type **01970**, press **[Enter]**, type **Road Bike**, press **[Enter]**, type **6/15/95**, press **[Enter]**, type **25**, then press **[Enter]**
The first record has been entered. Note that you can advance to the next field by pressing either [Enter] or [Tab]. Michael enters nine additional records.

6 Enter the additional records shown in Table 2-3
Don't be concerned about making mistakes; you learn how to edit records in the next lesson.

7 Resize the fields to the largest entry in the column

8 Click the **Save button** 🖫
Compare your table to Figure 2-13.

FIGURE 2-11:
Datasheet window and resizing pointer

Double-click to widen column to widest entry

FIGURE 2-12:
Resized fields

FIGURE 2-13: Records entered in Customers table

New record indicator

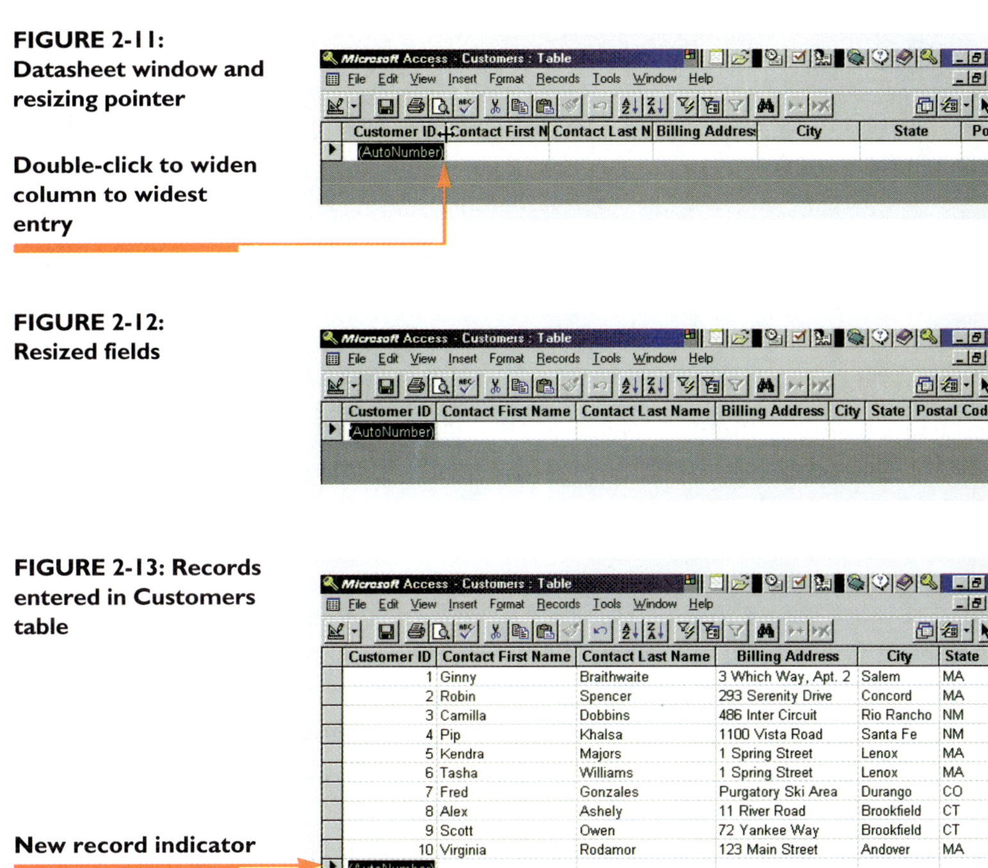

TABLE 2-3: Records in Customers table

CUSTOMER ID	FIRSTNAME	LASTNAME	ADDRESS	CITY	STATE	POSTALCODE	TOUR	DATE	AGE
1	Ginny	Braithwaite	3 Which Way, Apt. 2	Salem	MA	01970	Road Bike	6/15/95	25
2	Robin	Spencer	293 Serenity Drive	Concord	MA	01742	Mt. Bike	9/26/94	32
3	Camilla	Dobbins	486 Inter Circuit	Rio Rancho	NM	87124	Road Bike	6/15/95	30
4	Pip	Khalsa	1100 Vista Road	Santa Fe	NM	87505	Mt. Bike	9/26/94	28
5	Kendra	Majors	1 Spring Street	Lenox	MA	02140	Bungee	9/20/94	21
6	Tasha	Williams	1 Spring Street	Lenox	MA	02140	Road Bike	6/15/95	28
7	Fred	Gonzales	Purgatory Ski Area	Durango	CO	81301	Road Bike	6/15/95	26
8	Alex	Ashley	11 River Road	Brookfield	CT	06830	Road Bike	6/15/95	29
9	Scott	Owen	72 Yankee Way	Brookfield	CT	06830	Bungee	9/20/94	19
10	Virginia	Rodamor	123 Main Street	Andover	MA	01810	Bungee	9/20/94	22

Editing records

You can change the contents of a field at any time. To edit a field, you first click in the field, select the information you want to change, then type the corrections. You can use any text editing techniques. To cut or copy, select the text, then choose the Cut or Copy command from the Edit menu, place the pointer where you want the text, then choose the Paste command from the Edit menu. You can also use the toolbar buttons for Cut, Copy, and Paste instead of the menu commands. Table 2-4 lists several keyboard shortcuts you can use when editing records. For information on reorganizing columns in a table, see the related topic "Moving table columns." **case** After checking his records, Michael notices that he entered several fields incorrectly. He needs to edit the records to make the corrections.

I Double-click **Road** in the Tour field of record 7, then type **Mt.**
Notice that the Edit record indicator appears in the row selector for record 7. Michael also needs to change the date for this record.

2 Press **[Tab]** to move to and highlight the date, then type **9/26/94** and press **[Enter]** to change the date
Next Michael needs to correct the address information for records 5 and 6.

3 Click to the right of I in the Billing Address field in record 5, press **[Backspace]**, then type **530**
The Address field in record 6 should be the same as the Address field in record 5.

4 Press **[↓]** then press **[Ctrl]['']**
The address for both records is now 530 Spring Street, as shown in Figure 2-14. Michael saves the changes made in the table.

5 Click the **Save button** 🖫
When you modify the structure of a table or when you edit records, you need to save the table.

TABLE 2-4: Keyboard shortcuts in tables

SHORTCUT KEY	ACTION
[F5]	Move to a specific record
[F6]	Move between window sections
[F7]	Open the Spelling dialog box
[Ctrl][']	Insert the value from the same field in the previous record
[Ctrl][;]	Insert the current date
[Ctrl][=]	Move to the first blank record
[Esc]	Undo changes in the current field or record
[Shift][Enter]	Save the current record

FIGURE 2-14: Modified records

Edit record indicator

Field modified to match entry in previous record

Moving table columns

You can reorganize the columns in a table by moving them from one location to another. To move a column, click its field name so that the entire column is selected, then drag the pointer to the column's new location. As you drag, the mouse pointer changes to , as shown in Figure 2-15. A heavy vertical line represents the new location. Release the mouse button when you have correctly positioned the column.

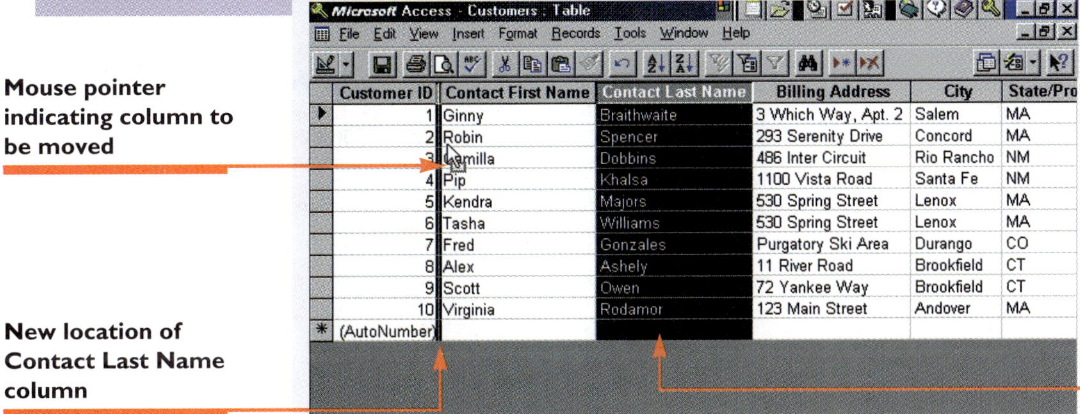

Mouse pointer indicating column to be moved

New location of Contact Last Name column

Column to be moved

FIGURE 2-15: Moving a table column

Previewing and printing the datasheet

After entering and editing the records in a table, you can print the datasheet to obtain a hard copy of the table data. Before printing, it's a good idea to preview the datasheet to see how it will look when printed and, if necessary, to make any adjustments to margins, page orientation, and so on. **case** Michael is ready to preview and print the datasheet.

STEPS

1 Click the **Print Preview button** 🔍 on the Database toolbar
The datasheet appears on a miniaturized page in the Print Preview window, as shown in Figure 2-16, and the Print Preview toolbar appears. Michael decides to use the Magnifier pointer to see how the datasheet looks when magnified.

2 Click anywhere in the miniaturized datasheet
A magnified version of the datasheet appears. Michael notices that several of the fields are missing. He returns the datasheet to its original appearance.

3 Click anywhere in the magnified datasheet
Michael decides to print in landscape mode in order to see all of the fields.

4 Click **File** on the menu bar, then click **Page Setup**
The Page Setup dialog box opens. This dialog box provides options for the way text looks on the page.

5 Click the **Page tab**, click the **Landscape radio button**, as shown in Figure 2-17, then click **OK**

6 Click **File** on the menu bar, then click **Print**
The Print dialog box as shown in Figure 2-18 opens, giving you several options described in Table 2-5. Michael does not have to make any changes to this dialog box.

7 Click **OK** to print the datasheet, then click **Close** on the Print Preview toolbar to return to the datasheet
With his printed datasheet, Michael is ready to save the table and exit Access.

TABLE 2-5: Print dialog box options

OPTION	DESCRIPTION
Printer	Displays the name of the selected printer and print connection
Print Range	Specifies all pages, certain pages, or a range of pages to print
Copies	Specifies the number of copies to print
Print to File	Prints a document to an encapsulated PostScript file instead of a printer
Margins	Adjust the left, right, top, and bottom margins (available through the Setup option)
Orientation	Specifies Portrait (the default) or Landscape paper (available through the Properties option)

FIGURE 2-16:
Datasheet in print preview (portrait orientation)

Close button

Columns missing from printout

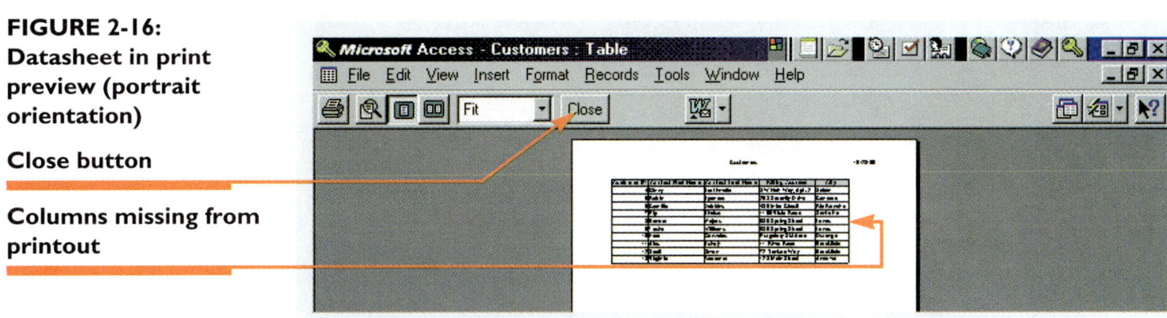

FIGURE 2-17:
Page Setup dialog box

Page tab

Click to display printout in Landscape orientation

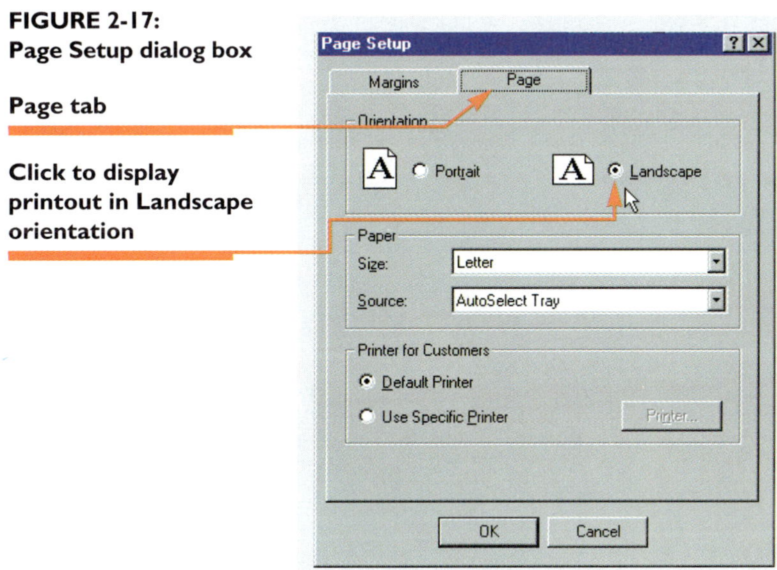

FIGURE 2-18:
Print dialog box

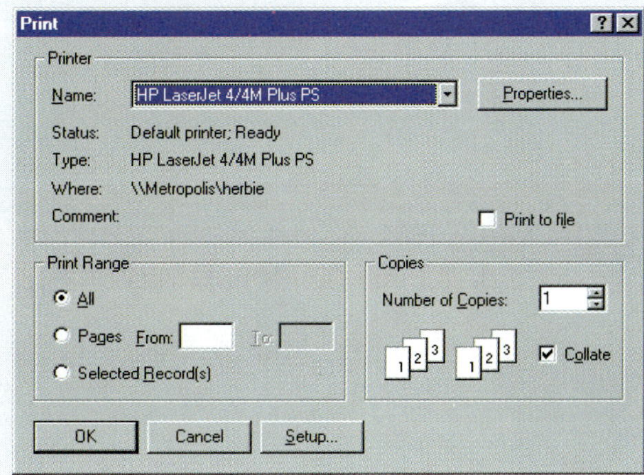

QUICK **TIP**

Click the Print button to print one copy of the entire datasheet without making selections from the Print dialog box.

TASKREFERENCE

TASK	MOUSE/BUTTON	MENU	KEYBOARD
Change field properties	Click Field properties area		[F6]
Create a database		Click File, New Database	[Ctrl][N]
Create a table	Click Tables tab, then click New	Click Insert, Table	[Alt][I], [T]
Datasheet view	, then click Datasheet View	Click View, Datasheet	[Alt][V], [S]
Design view	then click Design View	Click View, Table Design	[Alt][V], [D]
Insert current date			[Ctrl][;]
Insert value from previous record			[Ctrl][']
Modify a table	Click Tables tab, then click Design		
Move table column	Click field name, drag to new location		
Move to a record	Click a field in the record	Click Edit, Go To	[F5]
Move to first blank record			[Ctrl][=]
Open the find dialog box		Click Edit, Find	[Ctrl][F]
Preview datasheet		Click File, Print Preview	[Alt][F], [V]
Print datasheet		Click File, Print	[Ctrl][P]
Print datasheet in Landscape orientation		Click File, Page Setup, Page tab, Landscape radio button	
Print datasheet in Portrait orientation		Click File, Page Setup, Page tab, Portrait radio button	
Resize datasheet column	Double-click between field names	Select column, click Format, Column Width	[Alt][O], [C]
Save a Table		Click File, Save	[Ctrl][S]
Save the current record		Click File, Save	[Shift][Enter]
Undo changes in current field/record		Click Edit, Undo	[Esc]

CONCEPTSREVIEW

Label each element of the Access window shown in Figure 2-19.

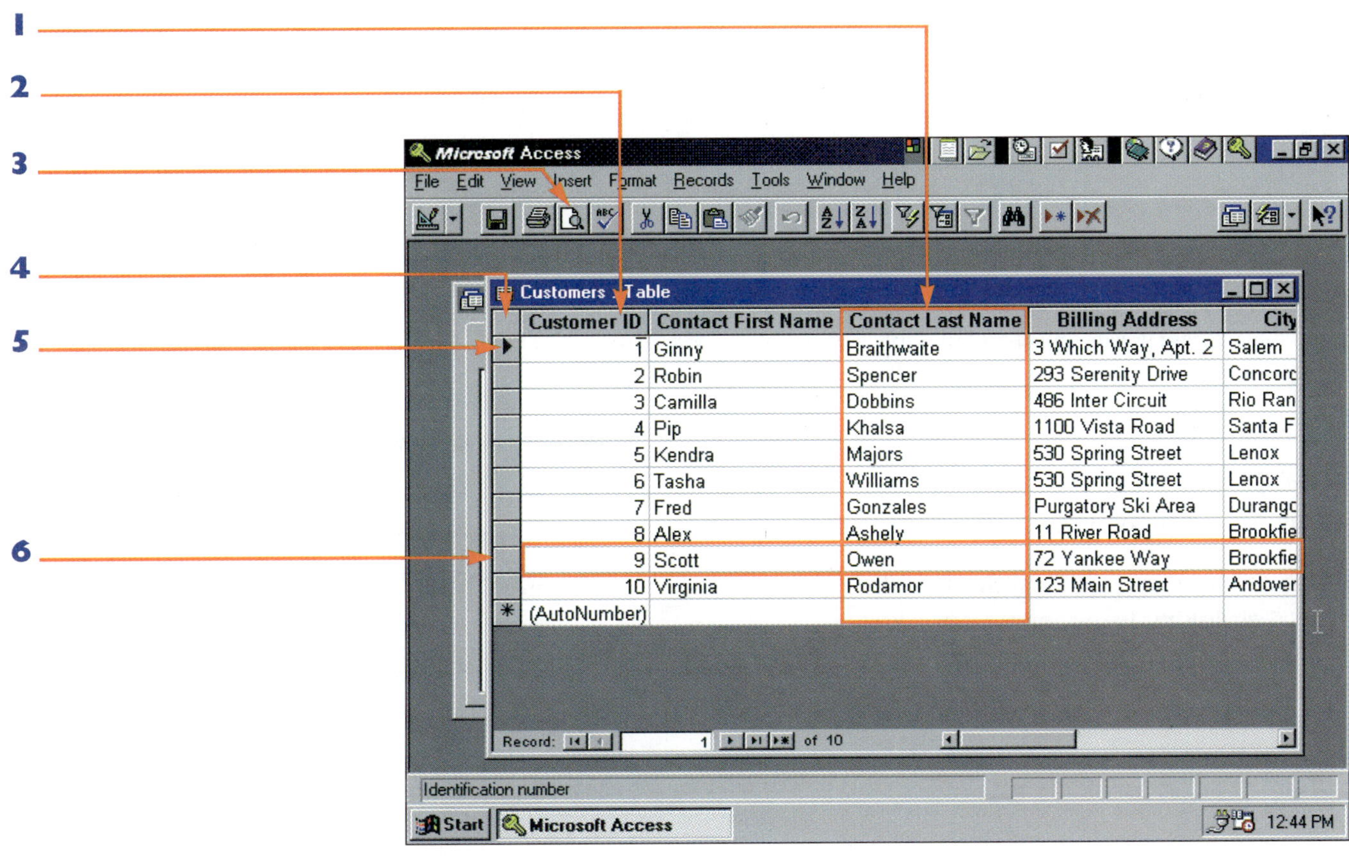

FIGURE 2-19

Match each data type with the statement that describes its function.

7 Numeric data type that automatically increases with each record

8 Alphanumeric characters of no more than 255 characters in length

9 Alphanumeric characters of unlimited length

10 Numeric values that can be used in calculations

11 Date and time values

a. Memo

b. Date/Time

c. Counter

d. Text

e. Number

Select the best answer from the list of choices.

12 All of the following procedures save a record except:

a. Pressing [Tab] to advance to the next record

b. Pressing [Shift][Ctrl] while in the record

c. Pressing [Enter] to advance to the next record

d. Pressing [Shift][Enter] while in the record

13 When the mouse pointer is placed between two field selectors, it becomes

a. ↖

b. ↔

c. (hand pointer)

d. ✛ or the Help pointer ▸?

14 Which data type would you use for a field that will contain phone numbers?

  a. Text

  b. Currency

  c. Number

  d. AutoNumber

15 The button that closes the Print Preview window is

  a. [Close button]

  b. [X button]

  c. [magnifier button]

  d. [printer button]

16 The Table Wizard provides all of the following, except:

  a. Sample tables

  b. Sample fields

  c. Sample field descriptions

  d. Business and personal tables

17 Which key(s) do you press to switch between the table design window and the field properties window?

  a. [Ctrl] [=]

  b. [F5]

  c. [Ctrl] [']

  d. [F6]

18 Which method can you use to copy data from one record to another?

  a. Select the field(s) you want to copy, click File on the menu bar, then click Copy

  b. Select the field(s) you want to copy, then click the Copy button on the Database toolbar

  c. Select the field(s) you want to copy, then press [Ctrl] [']

  d. All of the above

19 To edit the primary key in a database you select the primary key then:

  a. Press [Del]

  b. Press [Backspace]

  c. Click the Cut button on the Database toolbar

  d. None of the above

SKILLS REVIEW

1 Plan a database.

  a. Plan a database that will contain the names and addresses of your business contacts.

  b. Based on your own experience, decide which fields you need to include in the database.

  c. Write down the necessary fields with names and descriptions for each field.

2 Create a database.

  a. Start Access and insert your Student Disk in the disk drive.

  b. Use the Blank Database radio button to create a new database file.

  c. Save the file as Contacts in the My Access Files folder on your Student Disk.

3 Create a table.

  a. Click the Table object tab in the Database window, then click New.

  b. Use the Table Wizard to create the new table.

  c. In the Sample Tables list box, click Contacts. Make sure the Business radio button is selected.

  d. In the Sample Fields list box, choose each of the following fields for your table:
  ContactID
  FirstName
  LastName
  Address
  City
  StateOrProvince
  PostalCode
  Birthdate

  e. Continue through the Table Wizard. Name the table Business Contacts.

  f. Click the Modify the table design radio button in the third Table Wizard dialog box, then click Finish.

4 Modify a table.

   a. In the first available blank row, add a new text field called "Other."

   b. Click the ContactID field Description box.

   c. Type "Unique number for Contact."

   d. Press [↓] to move to the next Description box. Add appropriate descriptions for the other fields.

5 Enter records.

   a. Display the Datasheet window.

   b. Enter the names of 10 people you consider to be associates. You can make up the data if you want.

   c. Resize the columns so that all the data is displayed.

6 Edit records, then preview and print the datasheet.

   a. Make at least three changes to the records.

   b. Click the Print Preview button on the Database toolbar to display the datasheet in the Print Preview window.

   c. After viewing the datasheet, click the Print button on the Print Preview toolbar to print the datasheet.

   d. After printing, return to the Database window.

   e. Save the table then exit Access.

INDEPENDENT
CHALLENGE 1

As the personnel manager for Green Gardens Realty, you are responsible for maintaining an employee record for each employee. Currently, Green Gardens employs four salespeople, three secretaries, and one general manager. You need to create a database to contain the employee information. Although you can add other fields, the following fields must be included in your database table:

   EmployeeID
   FirstName
   LastName
   SocialSecurityNumber
   Title
   DateHired
   Salary

To complete this independent challenge:

1 Sketch a sample database on paper, indicating which fields are necessary. Write down each field name and a description of the field's function.

2 Create a database file named Green Gardens in the My Access Files folder on your Student Disk.

3 Use the Table Wizard to create the table, and use the Employees sample table to select the fields. Make sure the Business radio button is selected in the Table Wizard dialog box, and accept the default table name.

4 Make up data and add records for each employee.

5 Save the table, then preview and print the datasheet.

6 Close the table.

7 Submit your paper sketch with your printed datasheet.

INDEPENDENT
CHALLENGE 2

Create a database that catalogs your own music collection. Be sure to include the following fields, although you can add others:

MusicCollectionID
GroupName
Title
Format
YearReleased

To complete this independent challenge:

1 Sketch a sample database on paper, indicating which fields are necessary. Write down each field name and a description of the field's function.

2 Create a database file named My Music in the My Access Files folder on your Student Disk.

3 Use the Table Wizard to create the table, and use the Music Collection sample table (a Personal table) to select the fields.

4 Enter records for your music collection. Enter a minimum of 10 records.

5 Save the table, then preview and print the datasheet.

6 Close the table then exit Access.

7 Submit your paper sketch with your printed datasheet.

INDEPENDENT
CHALLENGE 3

The customer database for the Nuts and Bolts hardware store has been started but needs additional fields and field descriptions. Be sure to add descriptions to the existing fields, and add missing fields and descriptions using the following table as a guide.

Field	Description
CustomerID	A unique number for the Customer.
FirstName	The Customer's first name and optional middle initial.
LastName	The Customer's last name.
TelephoneNumber	The Customer's telephone number.
CreditLine	The Customer's in-store credit line.
PostalCode	The Customer's zip code.

To complete this independent challenge:

1 Open the file Nuts and Bolts Customers on your Student Disk.

2 Using the previous table as a guide, add the missing fields, as well as descriptions for all the fields.

3 Enter a minimum of 10 records. (You can make up the information.) *Hint:* Be sure to use the text data type for the phone number.

4 Save the table, then preview and print the datasheet.

5 Close the table then exit Access.

6 Submit your printed datasheet.

INDEPENDENT
CHALLENGE 4

Your local Chamber of Commerce has started to create a database which contains information of area businesses. Additional fields and field descriptions need to be added. Be sure to add descriptions to the existing fields, and add missing fields and descriptions using the following table as a guide.

Field	Description
CompanyName	The business' official name.
OwnerFirstName	The Owner's first name.
OwnerLastName	The Owner's last name.
TelephoneNumber	The company's telephone number.
FaxNumber	The company's fax number.
AnnualSales	The company's estimated annual sales.
PostalCode	The company's zip code.
BusinessType	The company's business classification.

To complete this independent challenge:

1 Open the file Area Businesses on your Student Disk.

2 Using the previous table as a guide, add the missing fields, as well as descriptions for all the fields.

3 Enter a minimum of 10 records. (You can make up the information.)

4 Save the table, then preview and print the datasheet.

5 Close the table then exit Access.

6 Submit your printed datasheet.

VISUALWORKSHOP

Create the following table using the skills you learned in this Unit.

FIGURE 2-20

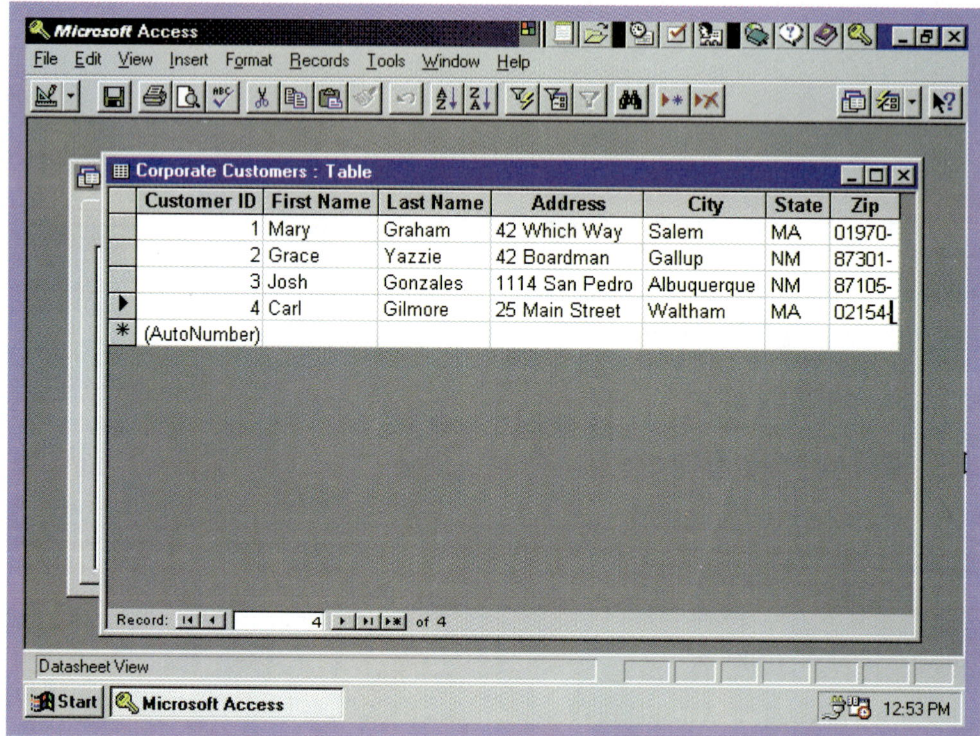

OBJECTIVES

- ▶ Find records
- ▶ Sort a table
- ▶ Filter a table
- ▶ Create a simple query
- ▶ Create a complex query
- ▶ Modify a query

Manipulating DATA

After you create an Access database table and enter data in it, you can manipulate the data easily to find the information you need. In this unit, you will learn how to find and organize data to display the results you want. You will also learn techniques for retrieving information from a table based on specified criteria. **case** Nomad Ltd's Travel Division uses its customer database to learn which tours are popular, as well as the demographic backgrounds of its clients. Michael created this database and entered all customer records in it. Now he wants to manipulate the data so he can include preliminary information on Nomad customers in the Annual Report. ▶

Finding records

Finding records in a table is an important database task. Table 3-1 lists a variety of keyboard shortcuts used to navigate a table. In addition, you can locate specific records using the datasheet. For information on finding records, see the related topic "Using wildcards in Find." **case** Michael wants to locate the record for Carol Smith because he entered her name incorrectly when creating the table; he needs to change the last name to "Smithers." Then he needs to enter a record for a new customer.

1 Start Access and insert your Student Disk in the disk drive

2 Click the **Open an Existing Database radio button**, click **More Files** in this list box if necessary, click **OK**, click the **look in list arrow**, click **3½ Floppy (A:)**, then select the database named Tour Customer Data and click **Open**
Next Michael opens the Customers table and maximizes it so it fills the screen.

3 Click the **Tables tab** in the Database window, click **Customers**, click **Open**, then click the **Maximize button** to maximize the table window
Access displays the Customers table, which contains 30 records, as shown in Figure 3-1. If the Table Datasheet toolbar is not displayed, continue to Step 4; otherwise skip to Step 5.

4 Click **View** on the menu bar, click **Toolbars** to display the Toolbars dialog box, click **Table Datasheet**, then click **Close**
Michael will use the Table Datasheet toolbar to change Carol Smith's last name to Smithers.

5 Click the **Last Name field**, then click the **Find button** 🔍 on the Table Datasheet toolbar
The Find in field dialog box opens, as shown in Figure 3-2. By default Access searches the current field, which in this case is Last Name.

6 Type **Smith** in the Find What text box, click **Find Next**, then click **Close**
Access highlights the name "Smith" in record 11, which is now the current record, for the customer Carol Smith. Michael can now replace the highlighted name with the correct name.

7 Type **Smithers**
Next Michael wants to see the last record in the table before he enters the new record.

8 Click **Edit** on the menu bar, click **Go To**, then click **Last**
The last name of the customer in the last record is selected. Next, enter the new record.

9 Click the **New Record button** 🔳 on the Table Datasheet toolbar, then enter the following data in record 31
Elizabeth Michaels, Mt. Bike, 6/20/95, 57 Beechwood Dr., Wayne, NJ, 07470, 38

FIGURE 3-1: Customers table

Table Datasheet toolbar

Number of current record

FIGURE 3-2: Find in field dialog box

Enter text needed to search for record here

Click to search all fields in table

Click to search for text exactly as entered in Find What text box

Using wildcards in Find

Wildcards are symbols you can use as substitutes for characters in text to find any records matching your entry. Access uses three wildcards: the asterisk (*) represents any group of characters, the question mark (?) stands for any single character, and the pound sign (#) stands for a single number digit. For example, to find any word beginning with S, type "s*" in the Find What text box.

TABLE 3-1: Keystrokes for navigating a datasheet

KEYS	ACTIONS	KEYS	ACTIONS
[↑], [↓], [←], [→]	Move one field in the direction indicated	[Tab]	Move to next field in current record
[F5]	Move to Record number box on the horizontal scroll bar, then type number of record to go to	[Shift][Tab]	Move to previous field in current record
[Home]	Move to first field in current record	[Ctrl][Home]	Move to first field in first record
[End]	Move to last field in current record	[Ctrl][End]	Move to last field in last record
		[Ctrl][=]	Move to first blank record

Sorting a table

Sorting Records

The ability to sort information in a table is one of the most powerful features of a database. **Sorting** is an easy way of organizing records according to the contents of a field. For example, you might want to see all records in alphabetical order by last name. You can sort records in **ascending order**, such as alphabetically from A to Z, or in **descending order**, such as alphabetically from Z to A. Be sure to view the CourseHelp for this lesson before completing the steps. ▶case Michael sorts his table in a variety of ways, depending on the task he needs to perform. His most common tasks require a list sorted in ascending order by tour, and another list sorted in descending order by date.

1 Click the **Tour field name**

The Tour column is selected. The table will be sorted by tour. In addition to clicking the Tour field name to select the field, you can also click any record's Tour field.

2 Click the **Sort Ascending button** on the Table Datasheet toolbar

The table is sorted in ascending order by tour, as shown in Figure 3-3. You can also sort records using the menu bar. See the related topic for more information. Michael decides to print this sorted table for reference using the default settings.

3 Click the **Print button** on the Table Datasheet toolbar

The sorted datasheet prints. Michael wants to return the table to its original order.

4 Click **Records** on the menu bar, then click **Remove Filter/Sort**

The table returns to its original order. You can also return a table to its original order by sorting the Customer ID field in ascending order. Michael's division wants to know which tour dates are popular, so Michael decides to sort the records in descending order by the Date field.

5 Click the **Date field name** to select the Date column

6 Click the **Sort Descending button** on the Table Datasheet toolbar

The records are sorted from most recent to least recent, as shown in Figure 3-4. Michael notes that bike tours are booming, with 18 customers taking bike tours in June of 1995. This information will be important in planning the 1996 and 1997 seasons. Michael wants to print the sorted table.

7 Click the **Print button** on the Table Datasheet toolbar

Next Michael returns the table to its original order.

8 Click **Records** on the menu bar, then click **Remove Filter/Sort**

FIGURE 3-3: Table sorted in ascending order by Tour field

Records sorted by tour

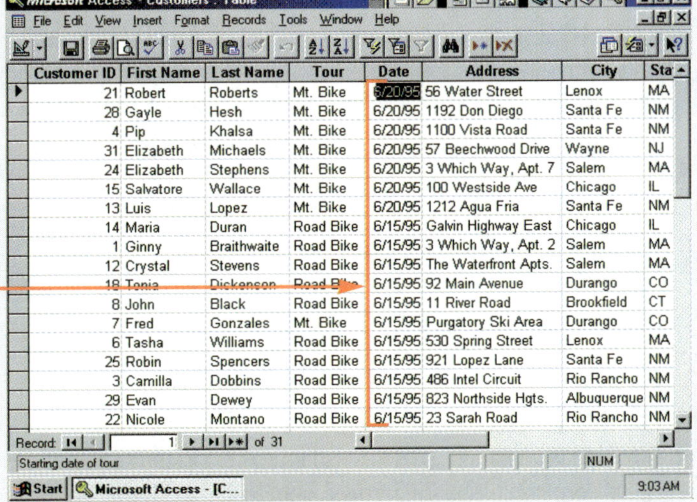

FIGURE 3-4: Table sorted in descending order by Date field

Records sorted in descending order by date

Using the menu bar to sort

In addition to using buttons on the Table Datasheet toolbar, you can also sort using the menu bar. After you select the field you want to sort, click Records on the menu bar, then click Sort. Click either Ascending or Descending on the Sort menu, shown in Figure 3-5.

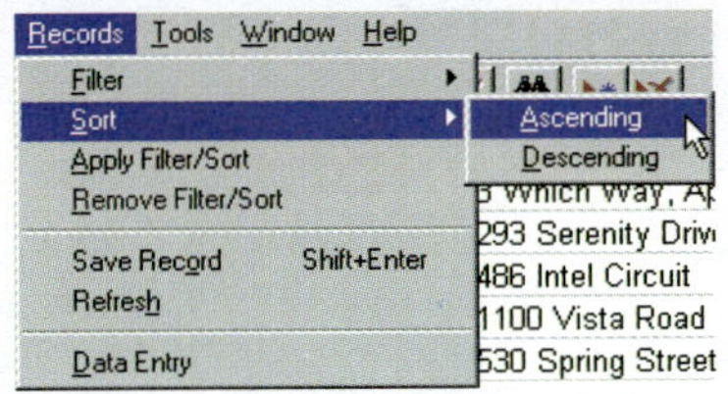

FIGURE 3-5: Sort menu

Filtering a table

Filtering Records

Sorting allows you to manipulate table records in a simple way and to display them in ascending or descending order. **Filtering** is a more complex method of organizing records where you define the fields on which the table is sorted. A sort contains all the records in a table, whereas a filter shows only those records that qualify, based on your **criteria**, or parameters. Be sure to view the CourseHelp for this lesson before completing the steps. See the related topic "When to use a filter" for more information. **case** Often, Michael needs a list of customers by a specific tour. He can filter the Customers table to obtain this list.

1 Make sure the Customers table is open, with all records displayed
Michael wants to narrow the number of records displayed so he can see only those records for customers who took a Mt. Bike tour.

2 Click **Records** on the menu bar, point to **Filter**, then click **Advanced Filter/Sort**
The Filter window opens, as shown in Figure 3-6. The **Filter window** consists of two areas: the **field list** on top, containing all the fields in the table, and the filter grid on the bottom, where you specify the criteria for the filter. If your filter grid already contains criteria, click the Clear Grid button ⊠ from the toolbar so your grid looks like Figure 3-6. The toolbar displayed is the Filter/Sort toolbar. Michael wants to create a filter to show an unsorted list of all the records of customers who took a Mt. Bike tour.

3 Double-click **Tour** in the field list
Access places the Tour field in the first empty Field cell in the filter grid. Next, Michael defines the criteria for the Tour field.

4 Click the **Criteria cell** in the Tour column, type **Mt. Bike**, then press **[Enter]**
Access adds quotation marks around the entry to indicate that the entry is text, rather than a value. Your completed filter grid should look like Figure 3-7.

5 Click the **Apply Filter button** ▽ on the Filter/Sort toolbar
Only those records containing the Mt. Bike tour appear, as shown in Figure 3-8.

6 Click **Records** on the menu bar, then click **Remove Filter/Sort** to return the table to its original order

FIGURE 3-6: Filter window for the Customers table

Field list

Field name goes here

Sort order goes here

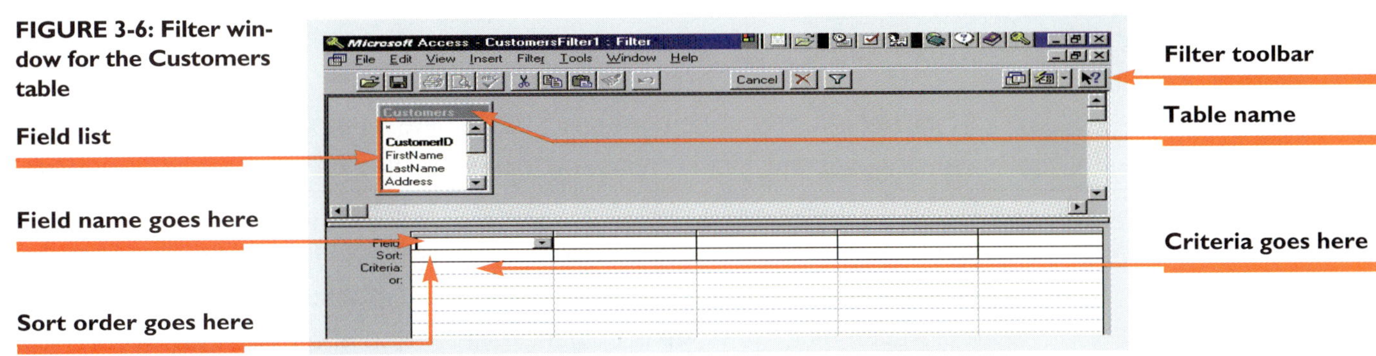

Filter toolbar

Table name

Criteria goes here

FIGURE 3-7: Completed filter grid

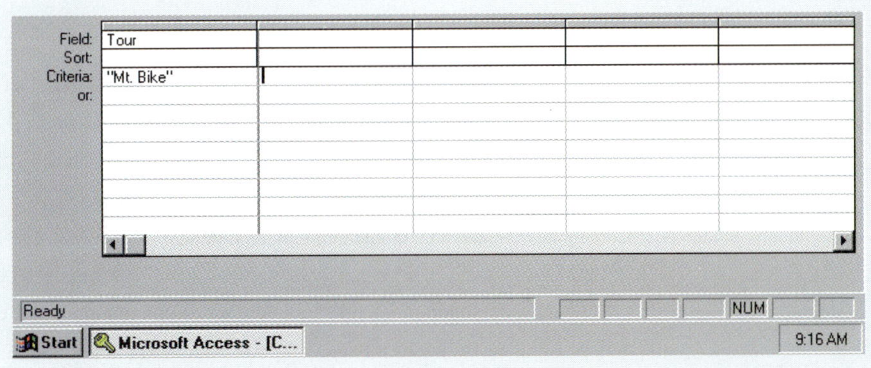

FIGURE 3-8: Filtered table records

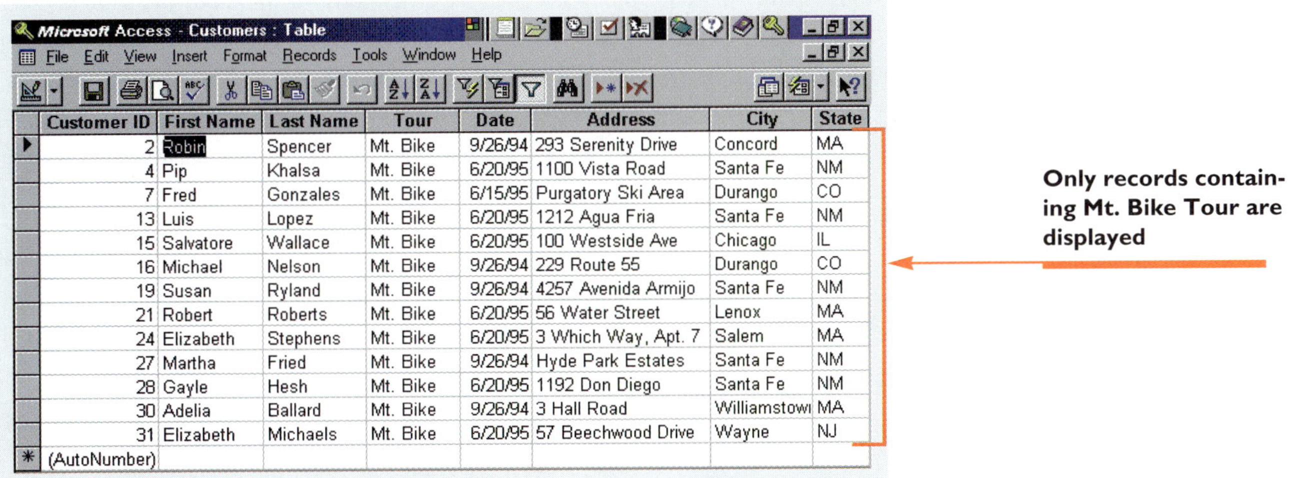

Customer ID	First Name	Last Name	Tour	Date	Address	City	State
2	Robin	Spencer	Mt. Bike	9/26/94	293 Serenity Drive	Concord	MA
4	Pip	Khalsa	Mt. Bike	6/20/95	1100 Vista Road	Santa Fe	NM
7	Fred	Gonzales	Mt. Bike	6/15/95	Purgatory Ski Area	Durango	CO
13	Luis	Lopez	Mt. Bike	6/20/95	1212 Agua Fria	Santa Fe	NM
15	Salvatore	Wallace	Mt. Bike	6/20/95	100 Westside Ave	Chicago	IL
16	Michael	Nelson	Mt. Bike	9/26/94	229 Route 55	Durango	CO
19	Susan	Ryland	Mt. Bike	9/26/94	4257 Avenida Armijo	Santa Fe	NM
21	Robert	Roberts	Mt. Bike	6/20/95	56 Water Street	Lenox	MA
24	Elizabeth	Stephens	Mt. Bike	6/20/95	3 Which Way, Apt. 7	Salem	MA
27	Martha	Fried	Mt. Bike	9/26/94	Hyde Park Estates	Santa Fe	NM
28	Gayle	Hesh	Mt. Bike	6/20/95	1192 Don Diego	Santa Fe	NM
30	Adelia	Ballard	Mt. Bike	9/26/94	3 Hall Road	Williamstowi	MA
31	Elizabeth	Michaels	Mt. Bike	6/20/95	57 Beechwood Drive	Wayne	NJ
(AutoNumber)							

Only records containing Mt. Bike Tour are displayed

When to use a filter

A filter is temporary and cannot be saved; however, you can print the results of a filter just as you print any datasheet. A filter is best used to narrow the focus of the records temporarily in the current table.

Creating a simple query

A **query** is a set of criteria you specify to retrieve certain data from a database. Unlike a filter, which only allows you to manipulate data temporarily, a query can be saved so that you do not have to recreate it. A query also displays only the fields you have specified, rather than showing all table fields. Records resulting from a query are collected in a temporary area called a **dynaset**, which looks like a table, but is merely a view based on the query. The most commonly used query is the **select query**, in which records are collected, viewed, and can be modified later. ▶**case**   The Nomad employee responsible for setting up Mt. Bike tours often asks Michael for a list of customers who have participated in these tours. Michael needs to create a query that displays the names of all Mt. Bike customers in ascending order. He does not need to see any other information.

1 Click the **New Object button list arrow** on the Table Datasheet toolbar, then click **New Query** on the pull-down palette
The New Query dialog box opens and displays options for using the Query Wizard and for designing a new query. Michael decides to design a new query.

2 Click **Yes** to save the table, click **Design View**, then click **OK**
The Select Query window opens, as shown in Figure 3-9. The Select Query window is similar to the Filter window; however, the Query Design toolbar provides more buttons than the Filter/Sort toolbar. Michael adds the first field, sort, and criteria specifications to the grid area.

3 Double-click **Tour** in the field list, then click the **Show box** if it is checked to deselect it
The Tour field name appears in the Field cell in the query grid. The Show box indicates whether or not the field will be displayed in the query results. Michael does not need to see the contents of this field—only the customer names. Michael does need to specify the criteria for the query.

4 Click the **Criteria cell**, type **Mt. Bike**, then press **[Enter]**
Michael wants the query results to show the last name, in ascending order, of each customer who participated in a Mt. Bike tour.

5 Double-click **LastName** in the field list, click the **Sort cell**, then type **a** (make sure the Show box is selected for the LastName field)
Typing "a" in the Sort cell displays the word "ascending" in the cell. Compare your grid to Figure 3-10. Michael wants to view the results of the query.

6 Click the **Datasheet View button** on the Query Design toolbar
The results of the query are shown in Figure 3-11. The results show that 13 customers took Mt. Bike tours. Michael returns to Design View.

7 Click the **Design View button** on the Query Datasheet toolbar
The query grid is redisplayed. Michael wants to save the query results.

8 Click the **Save button** on the Query Design toolbar, type **Mt Bike customers** in the Query Name text box of the Save As dialog box, as shown in Figure 3-12, then click **OK**
The query is saved as part of the database file.

9 Click **File** on the Query menu bar, then click **Close** to close the query

FIGURE 3-9: Select Query window

Query Design toolbar

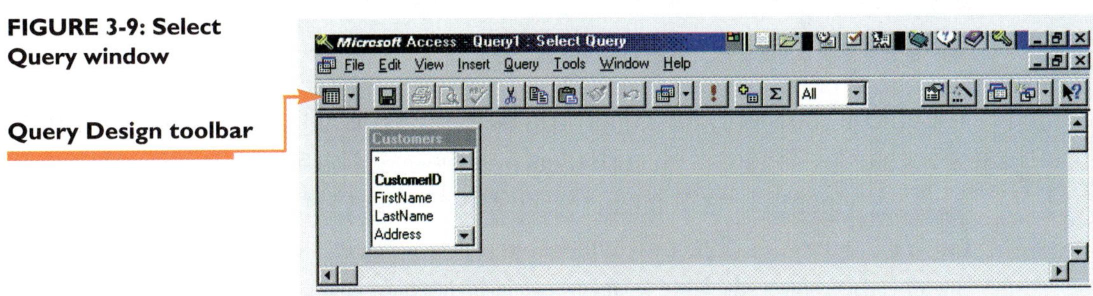

FIGURE 3-10: Sample query grid

Field data will not appear in query results

"ascending" appears when "a" is typed

Field data will appear in query results

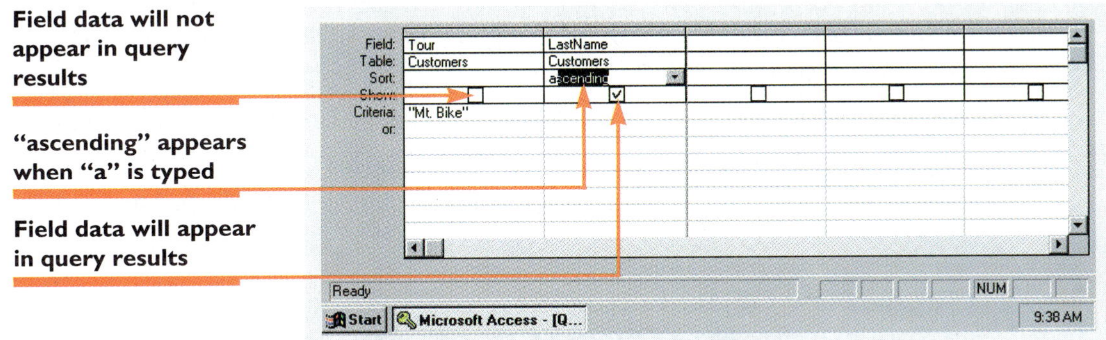

FIGURE 3-11: Results of simple query

Only Last Name field data appears

Number of records in results

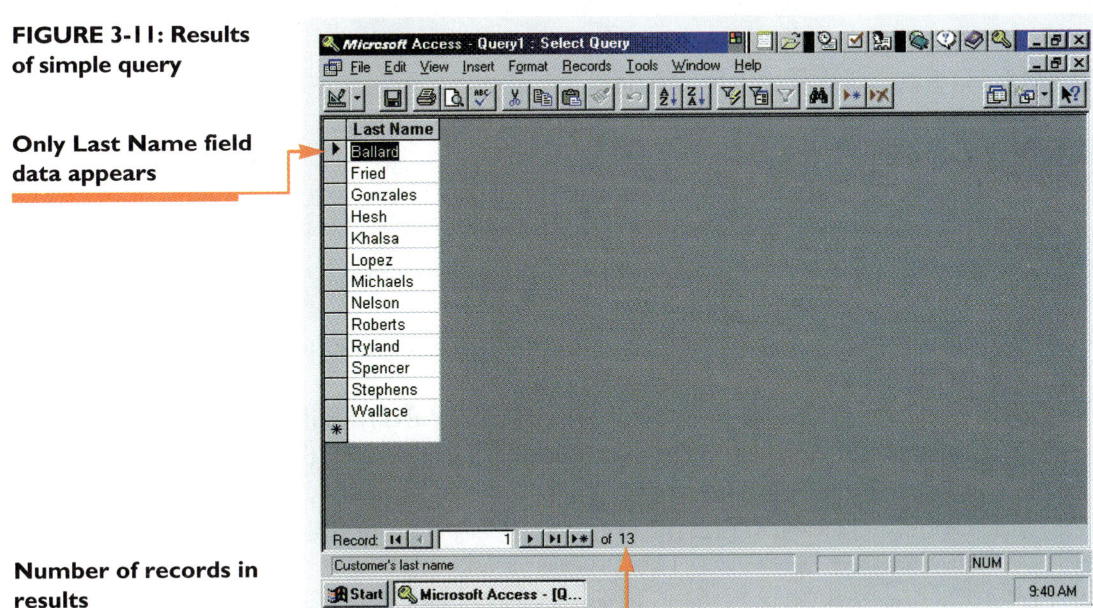

FIGURE 3-12: Save As dialog box for query

TROUBLE?

If you enter a field in the query grid in error, select the field then press [Delete] to delete it.

Creating a complex query

The criteria you specify for a query can be as simple as a list of all customer names, or as complex as a list of all customers over the age of 30, who live in New Mexico and took a tour in June. You can specify **AND** and **OR** criteria to broaden or narrow the number of records selected in a query. For example, a query of customers who took a Mt. Bike tour *or* a Road Bike tour gives different results from a query of customers who took a Mt. Bike tour *or* a Road Bike tour *and* live in New Mexico. Because a lot of thought goes into creating more complex queries, it is important that you save such queries if you plan on using them again. Table 3-2 lists the most commonly used Query Design buttons, which can help you design complex queries easily. ▶case   Each month, Michael wants to see a list of all customers, in descending order by last name, who took a Mt. Bike *or* Road Bike tour *and* who have a postal code greater than 50000. The list will also include the customers' first names. He decides to create and save a query that will display this data.

STEPS

1 Click the **New Object button list arrow** 🔲 on the Table Datasheet toolbar, then click **New Query** on the pull-down palette
The New Query dialog box opens. Michael decides to design a new query.

2 Click **Design View**, then click **OK**
The Select Query window opens. Michael adds the first field, sort, and criteria specifications to the query grid.

3 Double-click **Tour** in the field list
The Tour field name appears in the Field cell in the grid. Michael wants the tours displayed in ascending order.

4 Click the **Sort cell**, then type **a** to display the word "ascending"
You could also click the list arrow in the cell to display a list of choices, then choose Ascending. Michael wants the Tour field data displayed in the query results.

5 Make sure the **Show box** is checked
Michael wants to display the records of customers who took either a Mt. Bike or Road Bike tour. He enters this information in the Criteria cell.

6 Click the **Criteria cell**, type **Mt. Bike Or Road Bike**, then press **[Enter]**
The entry "Mt. Bike" OR "Road Bike" appears in the Criteria cell. See Figure 3-13. Next, Michael adds the FirstName and LastName fields to the query grid.

7 Double-click **FirstName** in the field list, then double-click **LastName** in the field list
The FirstName and LastName fields are added to the grid. Michael wants to sort the LastName field in descending order.

8 In the Last Name field click the **Sort list arrow**, then click **Descending**
With the OR criteria for the query specified, Michael decides to view the datasheet.

9 Click the **Datasheet View button** 🔲 on the Query Design toolbar
The results of the query are displayed in the datasheet. See Figure 3-14. Notice that customers who took either a Mt. Bike or Road Bike tour are listed. The last names are sorted in descending order and grouped by each tour type. Continue with the next lesson to complete the query.

FIGURE 3-13: "Or" specification in query grid

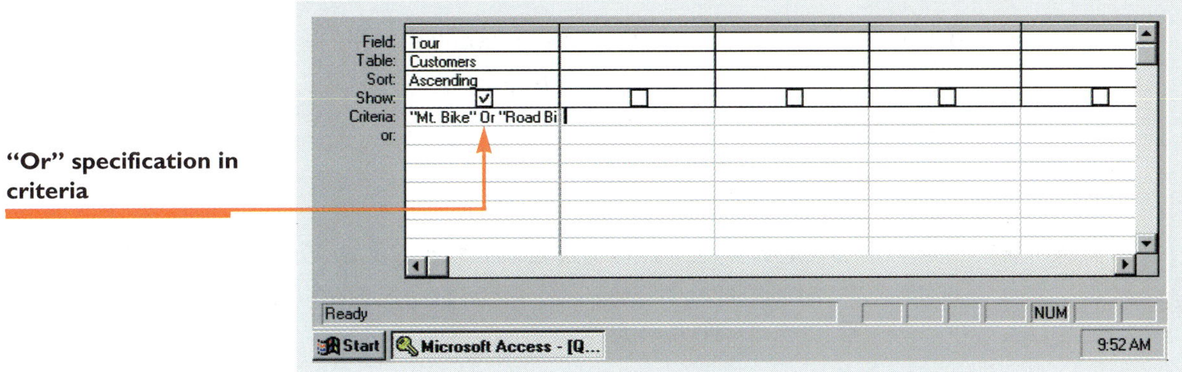

"Or" specification in criteria

FIGURE 3-14: Datasheet showing results of "Or" query

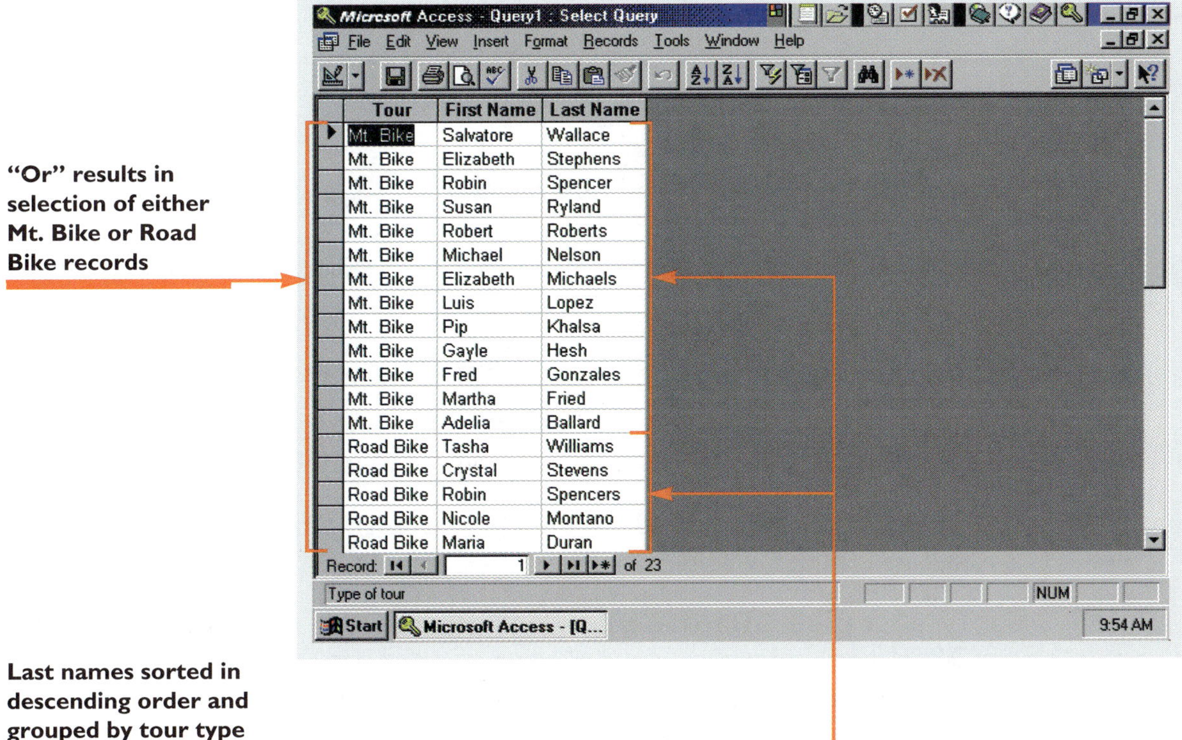

"Or" results in selection of either Mt. Bike or Road Bike records

Last names sorted in descending order and grouped by tour type

TABLE 3-2: Commonly used Query Design buttons

BUTTON	DESCRIPTION	BUTTON	DESCRIPTION
	Design View		Datasheet View
	Apply Filter/Sort		Sort Ascending
	Save		Sort Descending

Creating a complex query, continued

To complete his query, Michael needs to specify that the list include only those customers with a postal code greater than 50000. This is the "And" specification for the query.

10 Click the **Design View button** ![icon] on the Query Datasheet toolbar
The query grid is redisplayed. Michael adds the PostalCode field to the query grid, and does not sort it because the query is being sorted by the LastName field.

11 Double-click **PostalCode** in the field list
Next Michael adds the criteria for the PostalCode field.

12 In the PostalCode field, click the **Criteria cell**, type **>50000**, then press **[Enter]**
After you press [Enter], the Tour field might scroll out of view. If necessary, scroll the window to view the completed query grid, shown in Figure 3-15. Michael views the datasheet for the completed query.

13 Click the **Datasheet View button** ![icon] on the Query Design toolbar
The query results are narrowed from 23 records to 14 records with the addition of the PostalCode specification, as shown in Figure 3-16. Michael prints the datasheet so he can have a record of the results.

14 Click the **Print button** ![icon] on the Query Datasheet toolbar
Michael returns to Design view to save the query.

15 Click the **Design View button** ![icon] on the Query Datasheet toolbar

16 Click the **Save button** ![icon] on the Query Design toolbar
The Save As dialog box opens.

17 Type **Mt Bike OR Road Bike AND PostalCode > 50000**, then click **OK**
The query is saved for future use. Michael closes the query and the table.

18 Click **File** on the Query menu bar, then click **Close**; click **File** on the Datasheet menu bar, then click **Close**

FIGURE 3-15: Query grid with PostalCode field added

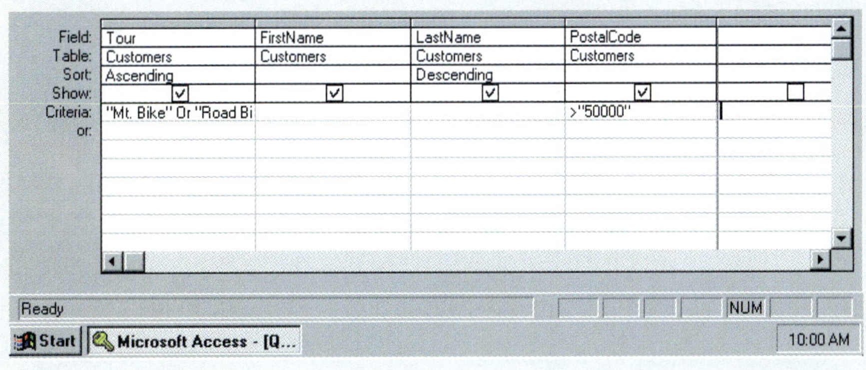

FIGURE 3-16: Results of complex query

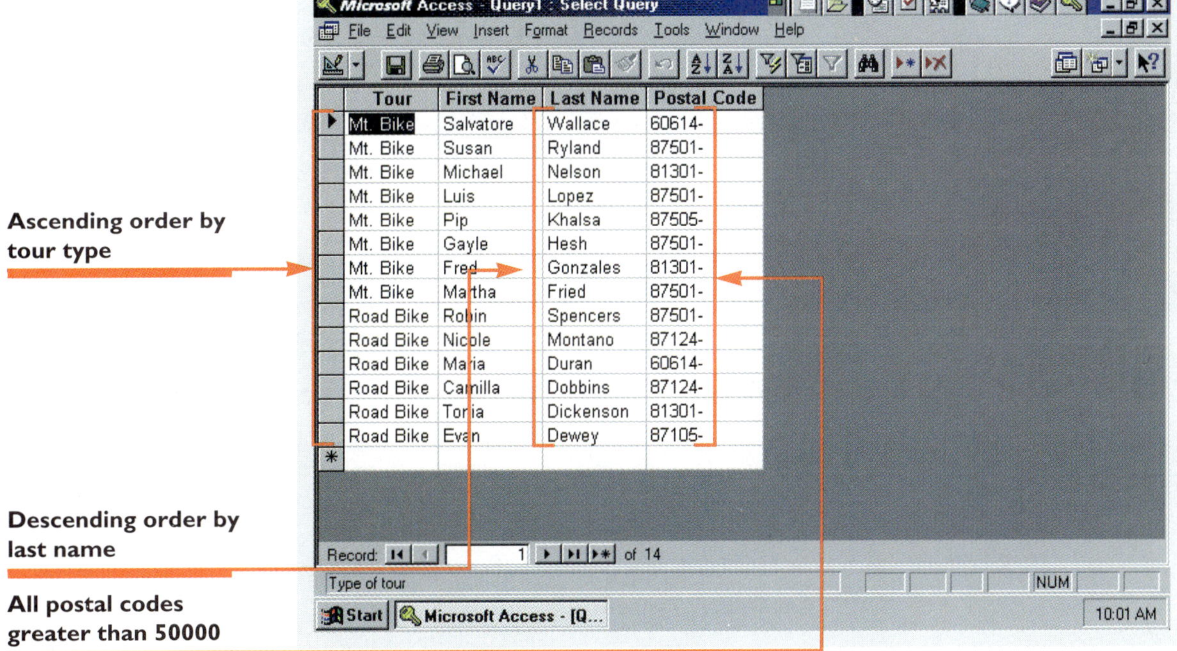

QUICK TIP

You can save a filter as a query by choosing Save As Query from the File menu (while in the Filter window), then name the query and click [OK].■

Modifying a query

After you create and save a query, you can modify it by adding and deleting fields, or changing field specifications. For example, you could change the sort order for a field or add new criteria for a field. When you modify a query you can save it with a different name. See the related topic, "Using Save As with queries" for more information. **case** Michael wants to add a field indicating customer age to the Mt Bike OR Road Bike AND PostalCode > 50000 query, and modify the sort specification for the LastName and PostalCode fields.

1 Click the **Queries tab** in the Database window, make sure the **Mt Bike OR Road Bike AND PostalCode > 50000** query is selected, then click **Design**

The Select Query: Mt Bike OR Road Bike AND PostalCode > 50000 window opens.

Michael wants to include the Age field in the query results.

2 Double-click **Age** in the field list

The Age field is included in the query for display purposes only. Michael will not specify any criteria for this field. Next, Michael needs to change the specifications for the LastName field so that it is not sorted.

3 Click in the LastName field, click the **Sort list arrow**, then click **(not sorted)**

Next, Michael changes the sort order for the PostalCode field to Descending.

4 Click in the PostalCode field, click the **Sort list arrow**, then click **Descending**

All the necessary changes have been made to the query. Compare your query grid to Figure 3-17. Michael needs to save his changes.

5 Click the **Save button** 🖫 on the Query Design toolbar

The query with modifications is saved. Now Michael views the results of the modified query.

6 Click the **Datasheet View button** 🖩 on the Query Design toolbar

The results of the modified query are shown in Figure 3-18. Notice that the Tour field data is still in ascending order, the LastName field data is no longer sorted, and the order of records within each tour type is sorted in descending order by postal code. The age of each customer is also displayed. Michael is finished with his modifications and returns to the Database window.

7 Click **File** on the menu bar, then click **Close**

8 Click **File** on the menu bar, then click **Exit**

FIGURE 3-17: Modified query grid

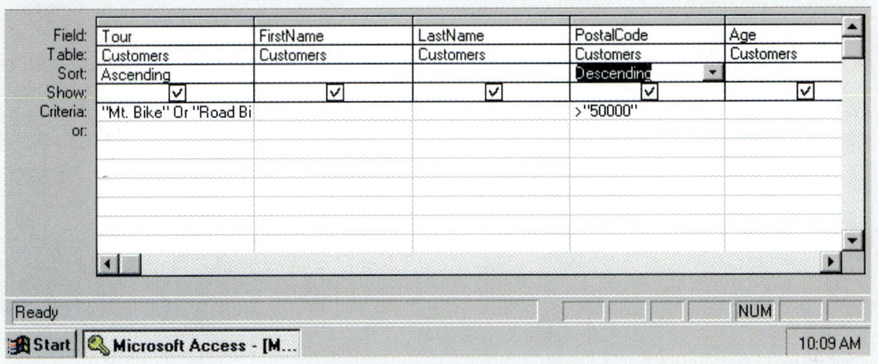

FIGURE 3-18: Results of modified query

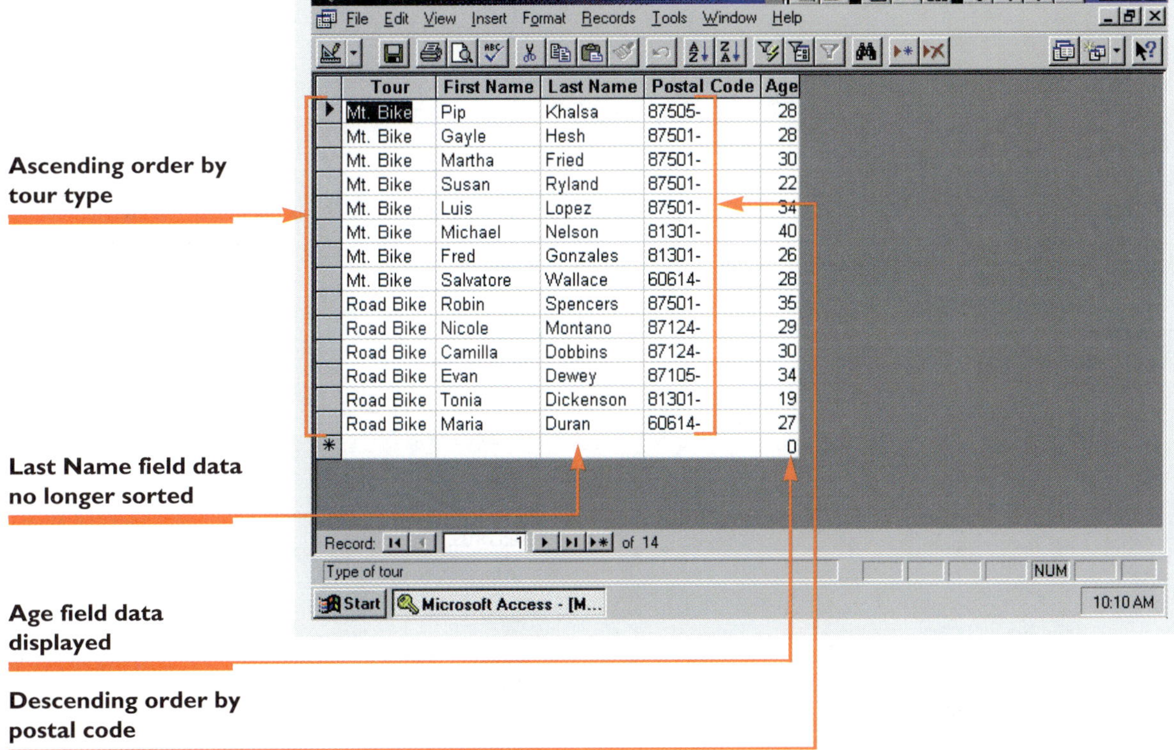

Using Save As with queries

You might want to create several queries that are similar. Rather than having to make minor adjustments in a query each time you use it, use Save As to create individual queries for each of your needs. Click File on the menu bar, then click Save As, and supply a new name for each query.

TASKREFERENCE

TASK	MOUSE/BUTTON	MENU	KEYBOARD
Apply a Filter	▽	Click Records, Apply Filter/Sort	[Alt] [R], [A]
Create a Filter using the Filter grid		Click Records, Filter, Advanced Filter/Sort	[Alt] [R], [F], [A]
Create a Query	▦ ▾, then click New Query		
Find text in a table	▥	Click Edit, Find	[Ctrl] [F]
Move to a record	Select current record number in navigation bar, then type desired number, press [Enter]	Click Edit, Go To	[Alt] [E], [G], ([F], [L], [N], [P] or [W])
Open a Database	▣	Click File, Open Database	[Ctrl] [O]
Open a Table	Click Table tab, click Table name, then Open		
Remove a Filter	▽	Click Records, Remove Filter/Sort	[Alt] [R], [R]
Return records to original order		Click Records, Remove Filter/Sort	[Alt] [R], [R]
Sort in ascending order	▲↓	Click Records, Sort, Ascending	[Alt] [R], [S], [A]
Sort in descending order	▼↓	Click Records, Sort, Descending	[Alt] [R], [S], [D]
Switch to Datasheet View	▤		
Switch to Design View	▨ ▾		

CONCEPTSREVIEW

Label each of the elements of the Select Query window shown in Figure 3-19.

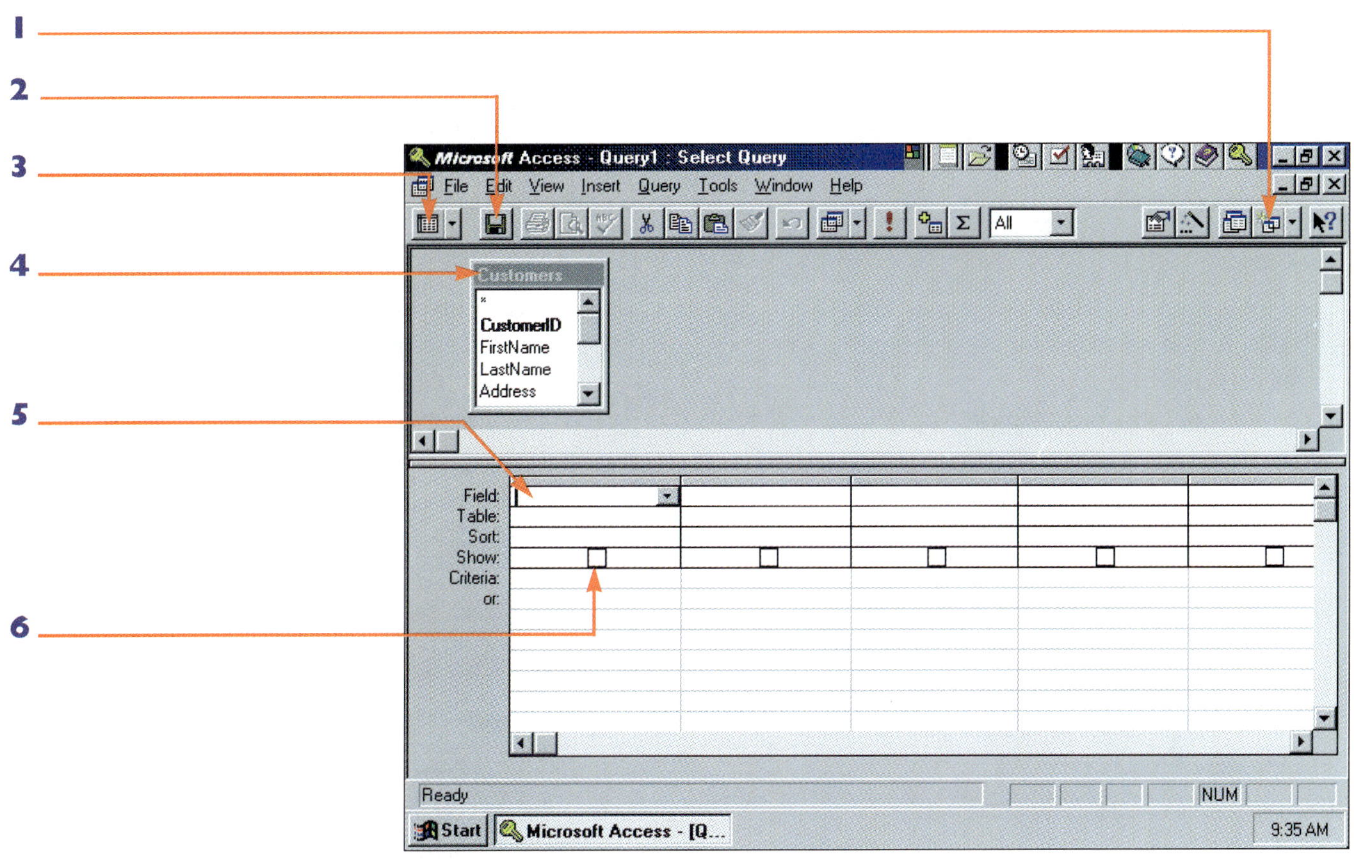

FIGURE 3-19

Match each button with its correct description.

7 a. Open Database

8 b. Print

9 c. New Record

10 d. Find

11 e. Datasheet View

12 f. Save

Select the best answer from the list of choices.

13 You can move to the first blank record by pressing

  a. [Ctrl][*]

  b. [Home][End]

  c. [Ctrl][=]

  d. [Home]

14 The button that sorts a table from A to Z is

  a.

  b.

  c.

  d.

SKILLSREVIEW

1 Find records.

a. Start Access and insert your Student Disk in the disk drive.

b. Open the database Bicycle Parts from your Student Disk. Open the Products table.

c. Use the Find button to locate all records in all fields that match any part of a field and contain the text "bar."

d. How many occurrences are there?

2 Sort a table.

a. Sort the Products table in ascending order using the Product ID field containing the five-digit numbers. Print the datasheet.

b. Return the datasheet to its original order.

c. Create and print a list of products in descending order by Units In Stock.

d. Return the datasheet to its original order.

e. Create and print a list of products in ascending order by Product Name.

f. Return the datasheet to its original order.

g. Create and print a list of products in descending order by Supplier ID.

h. Return the datasheet to its original order.

3 Filter a table.

a. Create a filter that shows all products on order. A product on order has a value larger than 0 in the Units On Order field. (*Hint:* Set the criteria in the filter grid to ">0" for Units On Order.)

b. Print the datasheet.

c. Return the datasheet to its original order.

d. Create a filter for all non-discontinued items.

e. Print the resulting datasheet.

f. Return the datasheet to its original order.

4 Create a simple query.

a. Create a query for Step 3a above showing only the Product ID field data containing the five-digit numbers and the product name for the items on order. Name this query "Products on Order."

b. Create a query for Step 3d above that shows the Product Name, Supplier ID, Units in Stock, and Unit Price. Name this query "Non-discontinued Products."

c. Create another query that lists all products with a unit price greater than $50. Name this query "Products costing >$50."

d. Display the ProductName, ProductID1, UnitsInStock, and UnitPrice field data in the query for Step 4b.

e. Create a query from the existing "Non-discontinued Products" query for discontinued products. Name this new query Discontinued Products.

f. Print out the Discontinued Products query.

5 Create a complex query.

a. Create a query that shows the Product Name of all products with a DiscoStatus = Yes field AND that are sold by the pair (the Units field). Sort the query in ascending order by units. Name this query "Discoed, by Unit."

b. Print the datasheet for the query.

c. Save the Discoed, by Unit query (created in Step 5a) as "Available, by Unit". Change the DiscoStatus = Yes field to DiscoStatus = No.

d. Print the datasheet for the query.

6 Modify a query.

a. Modify the Products on Order query so that the results are sorted in ascending order by the Supplier ID field. Make sure the Supplier ID field data is displayed. Save the modified query. Print the query results.

b. Modify the Products costing >$50 query to include the following fields: Product ID containing the five-digit number, Reorder Level, and Reorder Amount. Save the modified query. Print the query results.

c. Modify the Discoed, by Unit query so that the results are sorted in descending order by units, and so that the data for the Unit Price field is displayed. Save the modified query. Print the query results.

d. Close the file and exit Access.

INDEPENDENT
CHALLENGE 1

The Melodies Music Store has hired you as the customer service manager. You need to create queries in the store's music database, which is contained in the file Melodies Music Store on your Student Disk. The database includes one table, called Available titles.

To complete this independent challenge:

1 Using the Available titles table, find out how many records are in the Classic group. Should this classification be its own sub-group?

2 Sort the records by Category ID, then by Product Name. Print the results.

3 Create a filter that examines records with a Serial Number lower than 400000. Print this list.

4 Because musical categories overlap, group the eight classifications into three subgroups. You might, for example, group Alternative and Metal into a group called New Age; Classic, Pop, and Rock into a group called Rock N Roll; and World Music, Jazz, and Blues into a group called Easy Listening.

5 Create queries for each of the three subgroups. Each query must use an OR specification in the query grid. Name each query for its classification.

6 Query the Available titles table using each query, and print the results of each query.

7 Modify one of the subgroup queries to include a musical classification already included in another subgroup. For example, you could include Pop in Easy Listening as well as Rock N Roll. Print the results of the modified query and submit all printouts.

INDEPENDENT
CHALLENGE 2

You work in the US Census Office for your city. Using the database US Census Statistics from your Student Disk, create several queries that examine the data in the Statistical Data table. The records in the Statistical Data table contain marriage information by state.

To complete this independent challenge:

1 Add descriptions for each of the fields in the Statistical Data table.

2 Find the states in the same geographical area as your state. For example, if your state is Utah, other states in the Mountain Region are New Mexico, Colorado, Nevada, Montana, Arizona, Idaho, and Wyoming.

3 Create a query that selects records in your geographical area and sorts them in ascending order by state. Display the State and Marriages fields.

4 On paper, write down at least three additional queries that would extract meaningful data. Create each of these queries. Print a sample of each query's dynaset and submit each of the samples with the handwritten work.

INDEPENDENT
CHALLENGE 3

Your computer consulting firm has contracted to create a database for a special effects firm called Grand Illusions. Currently, Grand Illusions is working on five films, each having a minimum of 3 special effects they need to keep track of. Each special effect is created using some combination of computer imaging, prosthetics, multi-media, archived footage, and an in-house tool called Black Midnight.

To complete this independent challenge:

1 Create a database file on your Student Disk called Grand Illusions.

2 Create a table called Special Effects Register.

3 Create records for each special effect used in the five film projects. Each record should include the film name, special effect name, the Director's name, the tools used to create the effect, and the completion date of the effect.

4 Print the results of sorting the records in ascending order by film name.

5 Print the results of sorting the records in ascending order by completion date, then in ascending order by Director's name.

6 Create a query for each film which displays the completion date, Director's name, and the tools used, called YYYYYY Special Effects (where YYYYYY is the film name).

7 Print out each list and submit all printouts.

VISUALWORKSHOP

Use the Customers table in the Tour Customer Data file on your Student Disk to create the following output using a filter.

FIGURE 3-20

Customer ID	First Name	Last Name	Tour	Date	Address	City	State	Postal Code	Age
30	Adelia	Ballard	Mt. Bike	9/26/94	3 Hall Road	Williamstow	MA	02167-	42
13	Luis	Lopez	Mt. Bike	6/20/95	1212 Agua Fria	Santa Fe	NM	87501-	34
31	Elizabeth	Michaels	Mt. Bike	6/20/95	57 Beechwood Drive	Wayne	NJ	07470-	37
16	Michael	Nelson	Mt. Bike	9/26/94	229 Route 55	Durango	CO	81301-	40
2	Robin	Spencer	Mt. Bike	9/26/94	293 Serenity Drive	Concord	MA	01742-	32
24	Elizabeth	Stephens	Mt. Bike	6/20/95	3 Which Way, Apt. 7	Salem	MA	01970-	38

OBJECTIVES

▶ Create a form

▶ Modify a form

▶ Modify controls

▶ Use a form to add a record

▶ Create a report

▶ Modify a report

▶ Add an expression to a report

▶ Create a report from a query

Creating
FORMS AND REPORTS

The Datasheet View gives you an overall look at the records in a table. Often, however, all the fields in the table are not visible without scrolling left or right. Access allows you to create attractive screen forms that make it easy to view the fields in each record. You can design a screen form to match the design of a particular paper form to facilitate data entry. You can also create reports, which can display query results in different ways, both on the screen and in printed output. **case** Because Nomad Ltd's Travel Division has been so successful with its bicycle tours, it keeps an inventory of supplies, which it then sells to tour customers. Michael wants to create a form to make it easier to enter inventory data. He also wants to produce reports on the data to distribute to other Nomad employees. Michael plans to submit a sample form and report to the Board of Directors as part of the Annual Report. ▶

Creating a form

You can create a form from scratch, or you can use the **Form Wizard**. The Form Wizard provides sample form layouts and gives you options for including specific fields in a form. For information on creating a simple form automatically, see the related topic "Using AutoForm." 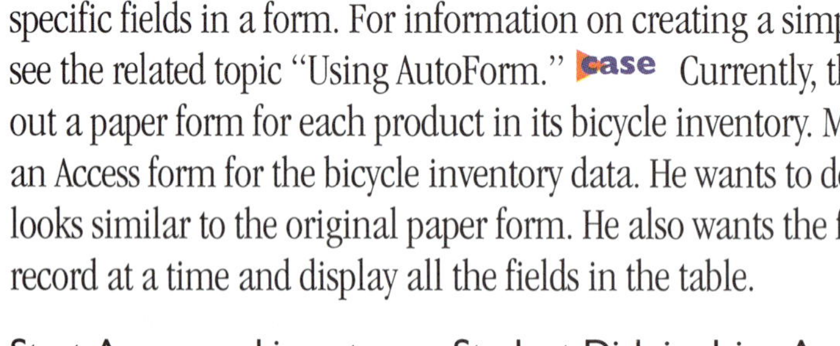 Currently, the Travel Division fills out a paper form for each product in its bicycle inventory. Michael needs to create an Access form for the bicycle inventory data. He wants to design the form so that it looks similar to the original paper form. He also wants the form to display one record at a time and display all the fields in the table.

1 Start Access and insert your Student Disk in drive A

2 Click the **Open an Existing Database radio button** in the Microsoft Access window, click **OK**, click the **Look in list arrow,** click **3½ Floppy (A:)**, click **Bike Inventory,** then click **Open**
This database file contains the bicycle inventory data. Michael wants to create a new form for the Bicycle Products table.

3 Click the **Forms tab** in the Database window, then click **New**
The New Form dialog box opens, as shown in Figure 4-1. Michael needs to identify the table on which the form will be based, then he can choose the Form Wizards option to create the form.

4 Click the **Choose the table or query where the object's data comes from list arrow**, click **Bicycle Products**, click **Form Wizard**, then click **OK**
A dialog box opens and lists all the fields in the table, as shown in Figure 4-2. This dialog box allows you to select which fields you want to include in the form, and to determine the order in which they appear.

5 Click **ProductID** in the Available fields list box, then click the **Single Field button** >
ProductID appears in the Selected Fields box. Michael wants all the fields to appear in the form. Instead of selecting each field individually, he decides to select all the fields at one time.

6 Click the **All Fields button** >> , then click **Next**
All the fields appear in the Field order on form box. Michael is ready to choose a layout for his form. He decides to accept the default style: a Columnar layout.

7 Click **Next**
Next, Michael chooses a style for his form. He decides to accept the default style suggested by the Form Wizard.

8 Click **Next**
The final dialog box suggests the table name as the title for the form. Michael accepts the title suggestion and wants to see the form with data in it.

9 Click **Finish**
The Bicycle Products form opens in Form View, as shown in Figure 4-3. The fields are listed in columns in the form, and the data for the first record in the table is displayed. The navigation buttons at the bottom of the form allow you to move from record to record, and the vertical scroll bar allows you to move to areas of the form that currently are not visible.

FIGURE 4-1:
New Form dialog box

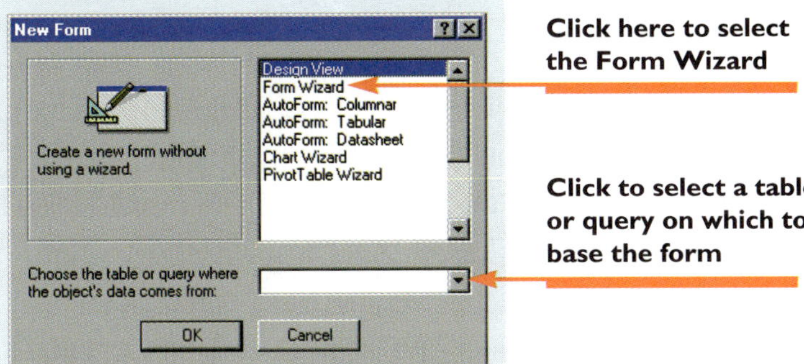

FIGURE 4-2:
Selecting fields in the Form Wizard dialog box

Places selected field on form

Places all available fields on form

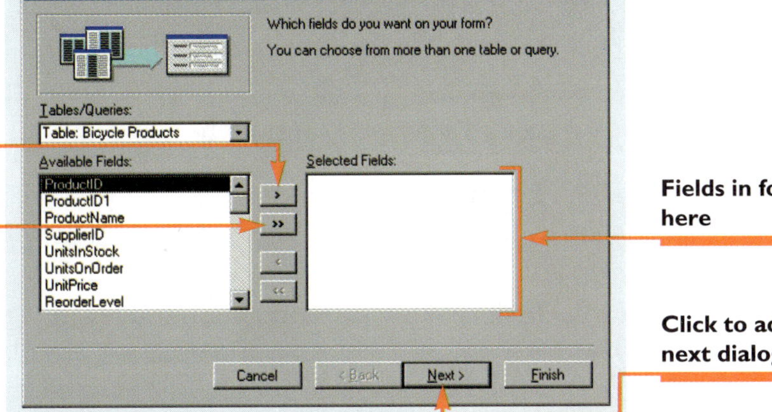

FIGURE 4-3:
Bicycle Products form

Fields in table

Navigation buttons

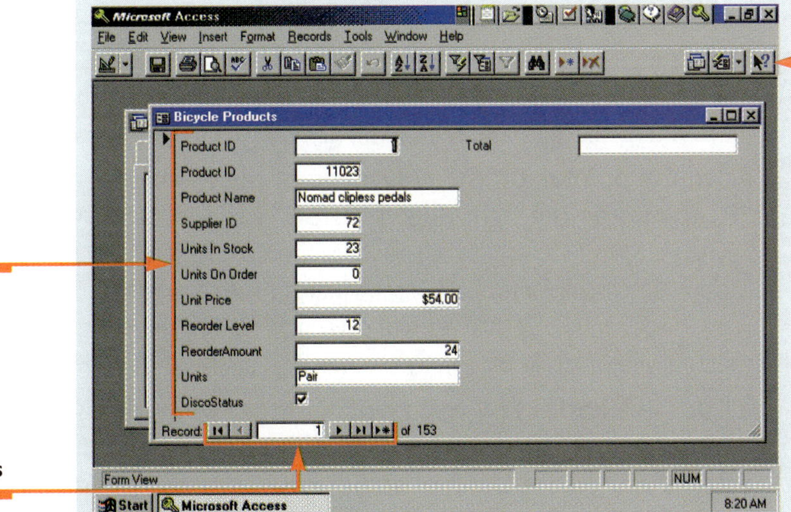

Using AutoForm

You can create a simple form by clicking the New Object button 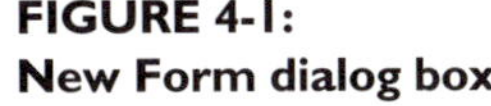 on the Database toolbar, then clicking AutoForm from the palette. AutoForm offers no prompts or dialog boxes; it instantly creates a columnar form that displays all fields in the table or query.

QUICK **TIP**

The Back button in the Form Wizard dialog boxes allows you to move to the previous dialog box and make changes, as necessary, before completing the form.

Modifying a form

After you create a form, you can modify it easily by changing the locations of fields, adding or deleting fields, adding graphics, and changing the color of text and field data. You modify a form in Design View, which is divided into three sections: Form Header, Detail, and Form Footer. The **Form Header** appears at the beginning of each screen form and can contain an additional form title or logo. The **Detail** displays the fields and data for each record. The **Form Footer** appears at the bottom of each screen form and can contain totals, instructions, or command buttons. In Design View, a field is called a control. A **control** consists of the field text and the data it contains. ▶**ase** Michael wants to reposition the fields in the form to match the design of the paper form. This will make it easier to enter data from the paper-based forms into the screen form. Figure 4-4 shows a completed paper form.

1 Click the **Maximize button** to maximize the Bicycle Products form
Maximizing the form gives Michael a larger work area in which to change the form design. Next he changes to Design View, where he can make modifications.

2 Click the **Design View button** on the Form View toolbar
The screen changes to Design View, as shown in Figure 4-5. (You might need to use the scroll bars to see the Form Footer section.) The form background changes to a grid, which helps keep fields aligned horizontally and vertically. The **Toolbox toolbar**, which might appear in a different area on your screen, contains buttons you can use to modify the form. Notice that each field name is displayed twice: the name on the left is a label that identifies the field; and the name on the right is the control for the field, which represents where the actual data for the field will be displayed. Before moving any fields, Michael wants to expand the size of the work area by placing the pointer on the right edge of the form, as shown in Figure 4-5, and dragging to the right.

3 Place the pointer on the right edge of the form until the pointer changes to ✛, then drag the right edge to the 6" mark on the ruler
Michael is ready to reposition fields on the form. To do this, he first needs to **select** a field by clicking the control for the field. Black squares, called **handles**, appear around the perimeter of a selected control. You can reposition a control by dragging a handle to a new location. When you work with controls, the pointer assumes different shapes, which are described in Table 4-1.

4 Click the **ProductName control** then, when the pointer is ✋, drag the control to the right of the ProductID1 control at 2.5" on the horizontal ruler, then release the mouse button
The Product Name field is now on the same line as the ProductID1 field as shown in Figure 4-6.

TABLE 4-1: Mouse pointer shapes

SHAPE	ACTION	SHAPE	ACTION
▷	Selects a control	✋	Moves the control where pointer is currently positioned
✋	Moves all selected controls	↔	Changes a control's size

FIGURE 4-4:
Bicycle Products
paper form

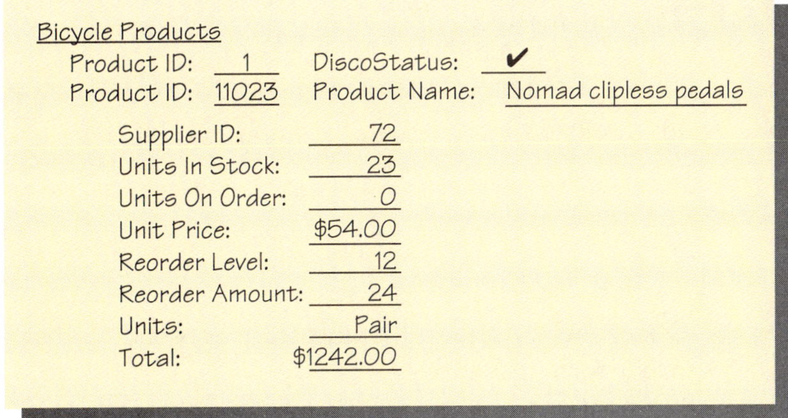

FIGURE 4-5: Bicycle Products form in Design View

Form Design toolbar

Detail section

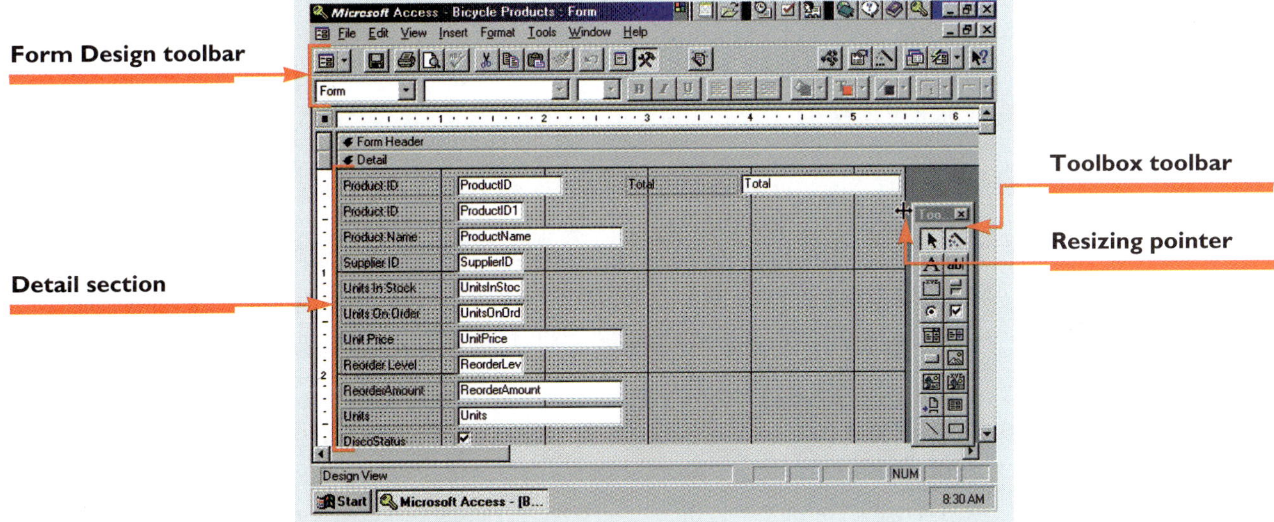

Toolbox toolbar

Resizing pointer

FIGURE 4-6:
Bicycle Products
form with enlarged
work area and relo-
cated control

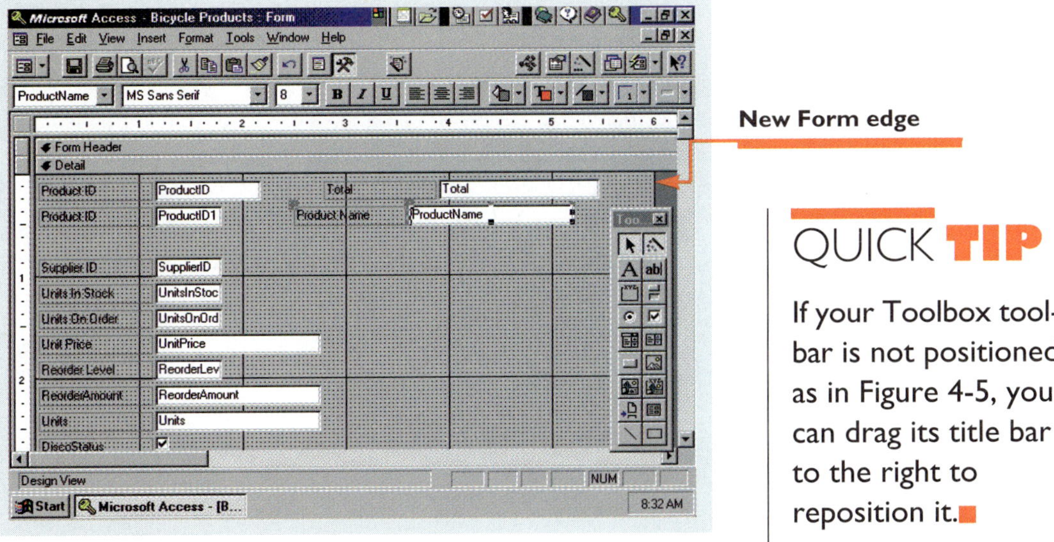

New Form edge

QUICK **TIP**

If your Toolbox tool-
bar is not positioned
as in Figure 4-5, you
can drag its title bar
to the right to
reposition it. ■

Modifying a form, continued

Michael continues to move controls so that all fields are visible on the form, and the screen form matches the paper form in Figure 4-4.

5 Select and reposition the necessary controls so that your form matches the paper form in Figure 4-4

You might need to use the scroll bar to see the remaining controls. Next, Michael needs to determine the tab order for the form. The **tab order** is the order in which you advance from one field to the next when you press [Tab] to enter data in the form. The order of the fields in a table determines the default tab order. Even when controls are repositioned in a form, the tab order remains in the original order of the fields in the table. Michael wants the tab order to reflect the order in which the fields now appear on the form, which matches the paper form, to facilitate data entry from the paper form.

6 Click **View** on the menu bar, then click **Tab Order**

The Tab Order dialog box opens. In this dialog box you can change the order of fields in any of the three sections on the form. Because fields are usually in the Detail section, this section is automatically selected. The Custom Order list box shows the current tab order, which still reflects the order of the fields in the table. Michael needs to change the tab order so that the DiscoStatus field follows the Product ID field, to match the new arrangement of fields in the form. The DiscoStatus field indicates whether the product is currently offered or has been discontinued.

7 Click the **DiscoStatus row selector** in the Custom Order list box, drag it until it is below ProductID, as shown in Figure 4-8, then release the mouse button

You can also click the Auto Order button in the Tab Order dialog box to rearrange the tab order to left-to-right, top-to-bottom.

8 Click **OK**

Although nothing visibly changes on the form, the tab order changes to reflect the order of the fields on the form. When Michael uses the screen form to enter data from a paper form, the order in which he moves from field to field by pressing [Tab] will match the order in the paper form. Michael saves his work and views the form in Form View.

9 Click the **Save button** 🖫 on the Form Design toolbar, then click the **Form View button** 🖃 on the Form Design toolbar

The form is saved as part of the database file. Compare your form to Figure 4-9.

Handles

Selected control

FIGURE 4-7: Repositioned controls

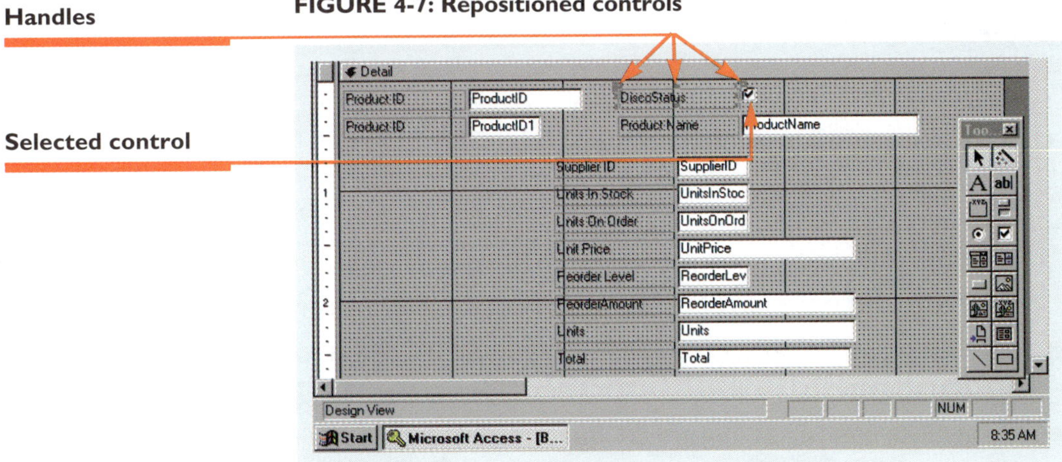

FIGURE 4-8: Tab Order dialog box

Indicates form section being displayed

Row selectors

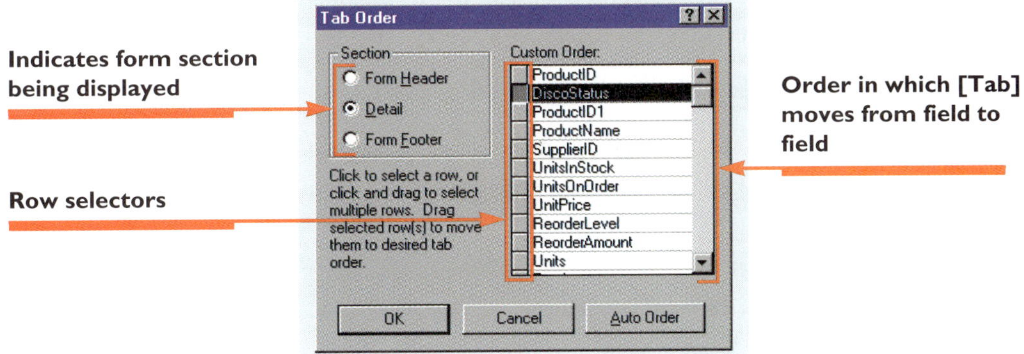

Order in which [Tab] moves from field to field

FIGURE 4-9: Form displayed in Form View

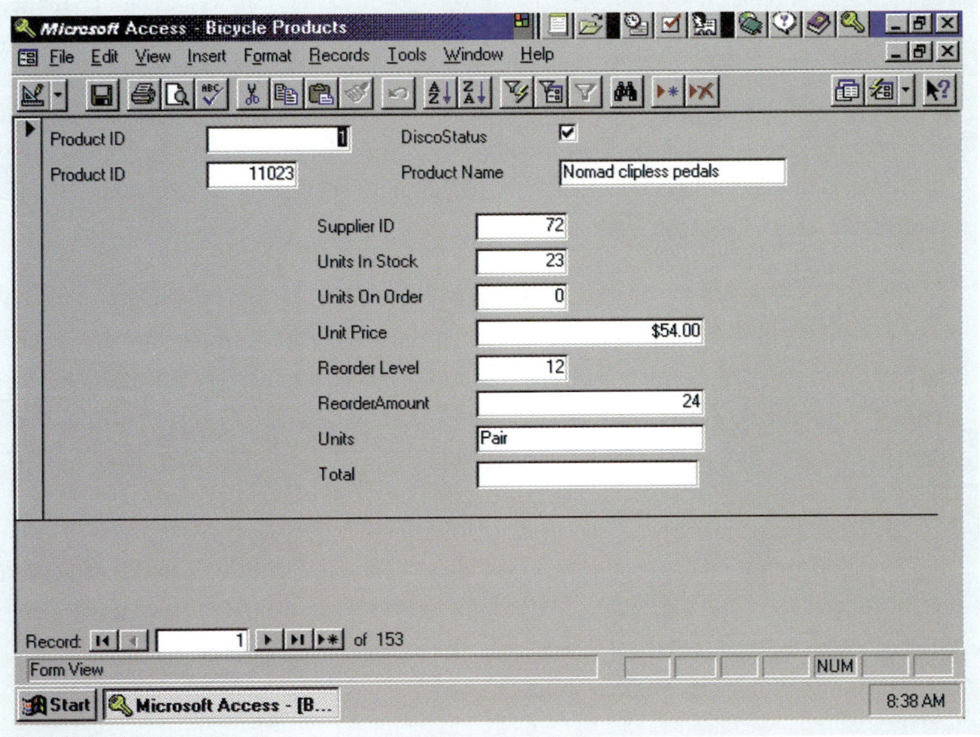

TROUBLE?

If the pointer changes to an I you will rename the field rather than move it. Click outside the field and try again. ∎

Modifying Controls

In addition to repositioning controls, you can also modify the **properties**, or characteristics, of a control to make data entry more efficient. Controls are either bound, unbound, or calculated. A **bound control** has a field in a table or query as its source of data. An **unbound control** has no source for its data (for example, an unbound control could be a title above a group of controls). A **calculated control** has a mathematical expression as its data source. By default, all controls occur as text boxes; however, you can create several types of controls, including toggle buttons and check boxes, using the Toolbox. See the related topic "Formatting a control" for information on enhancing a control. ▶**case** Michael wants to create a calculated control that will display an in-stock value for each item in the inventory. To do this, he will use the Expression Builder to create an equation that multiplies the Units In Stock field value by the Unit Price field value. The **Expression Builder** displays fields and mathematical symbols you can use to create an expression. First, Michael returns to Design View.

1 Click the **Design View button** 🖎 on the Form View toolbar
Michael wants the results of the expression to appear in the Total field. He must select the control for this field before creating the equation.

2 Click the **Total control**
Handles appear around the control to indicate it is selected. Although Michael could type an expression directly into the text box, he chooses to use the Expression Builder. You access the Expression Builder through the Properties Sheet.

3 Click **View** on the menu bar, then click **Properties**
The Properties Sheet opens for the Total control. The Properties Sheet shows the control's name and source, the field description as it appears in the status bar, and other relevant information. Because Michael wants to change the Total control to a calculated control, he needs to modify the Control Source property.

4 Click the **Data tab** in the Total Property Sheet
The Expression Builder's Build button displays, as shown in Figure 4-10.

5 Click the **Build button** 🔳
The Expression Builder dialog box opens, as shown in Figure 4-11. This dialog box contains a section in which you build the expression, the buttons you use to build the expression, and the fields available in the selected table. The word "Total" appears in the expression list box because that control was selected. Before building the expression, Michael must erase the word Total.

6 Press **[Backspace]** five times to erase Total
The expression will multiply the Units In Stock field value by the Unit Price field value.

7 Click the **Equals button** 🔳, double-click **UnitsInStock**, click the **Multiplication button** 🔳, then double-click **UnitPrice**
The completed expression appears in the expression text box. See Figure 4-12. If your expression does not match the one in the figure, use [Backspace] to erase the expression, then repeat Step 7.

8 Click **OK** to return to the Properties Sheet for the Total control
Note that the Control Source property shows the expression as the source for the Total control. Continue with the next lesson to finish modifying the controls.

FIGURE 4-10: Properties Sheet for Total control

Field name and
description appear
in the Format tab

Build button

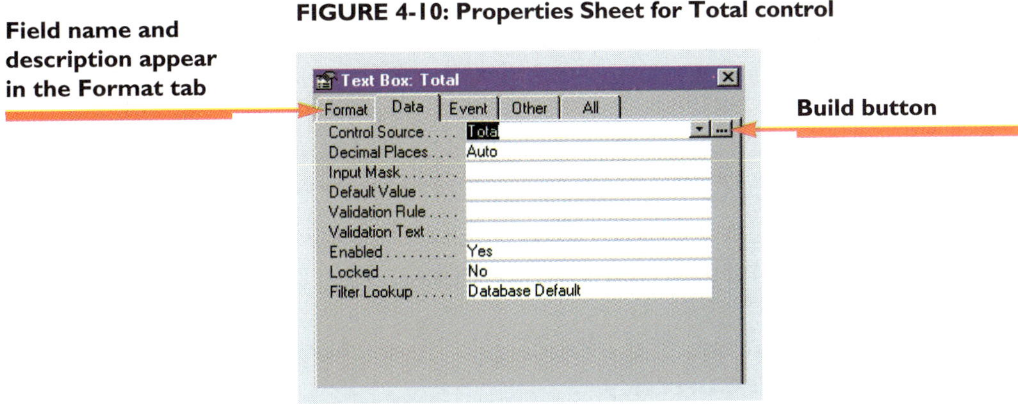

FIGURE 4-11: Expression Builder dialog box

Expression
appears here

Expression buttons

Current table

Available fields in
current table — you'll
need to scroll to see
all of them

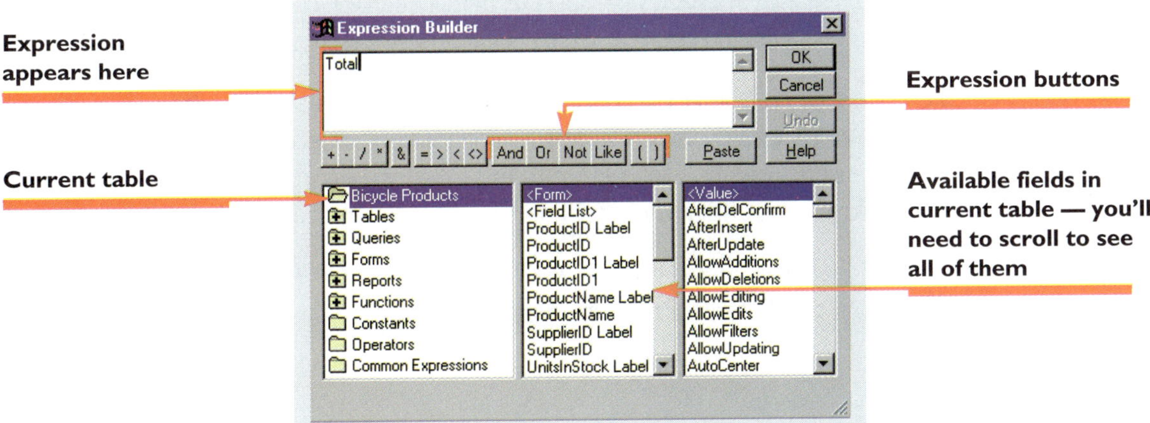

FIGURE 4-12: Completed Expression Builder dialog box

Completed expression

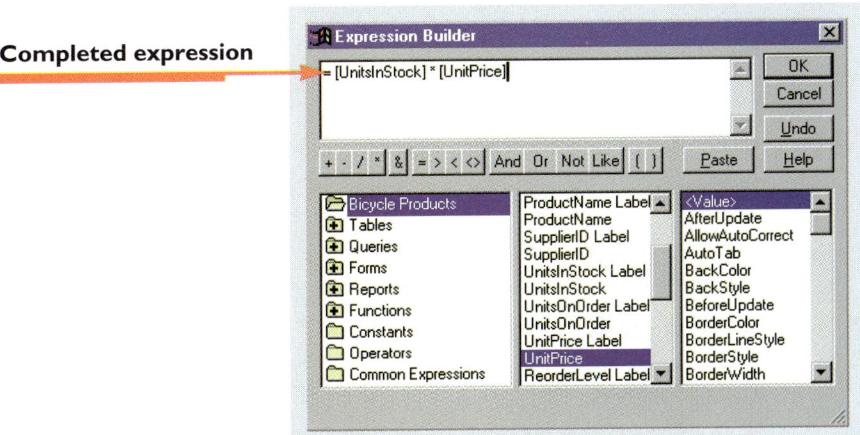

Formatting a control

You can bold, italicize, or underline a control by selecting it then clicking the
appropriate attribute button on the Form Design toolbar. You can use these attrib-
utes to make your forms more attractive.

Modifying controls, continued

Michael wants the calculated value to be displayed with the Currency format, which specifies a dollar sign, two decimal places, and commas separating thousands. Changing the format of a field's control only affects the appearance of the field data in the form; it does not affect how data is stored in the database. For more information on modifying controls, see the related topic "Aligning controls."

9 Click the **Format tab** in the Properties Sheet, click the **Format list arrow**, then click **Currency**

The Format property now specifies the Currency format. See Figure 4-13.

10 Click the **Close button** on the Properties Sheet window to close it

The form is displayed in Design View. Note that the equation you created using the Expression Builder appears in the Total control. Michael wants to view the completed form in Form View.

11 Click the **Form View button** on the Form Design toolbar

Compare your completed form to Figure 4-14. Don't worry if your controls are spaced differently. The calculated result of the Total field for the first record appears in Currency format. Michael closes the form, saving his modifications, and returns to the Database window.

12 Click **File** on the menu bar, click **Close**, then click **Yes** to save the changes to the Bicycle Products form

FIGURE 4-13:
Completed Properties
Sheet

Format changed
to Currency

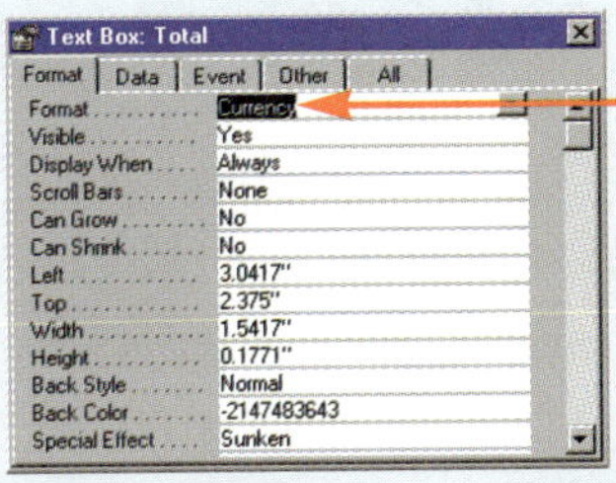

FIGURE 4-14:
Completed form in
Form View

Result of expression

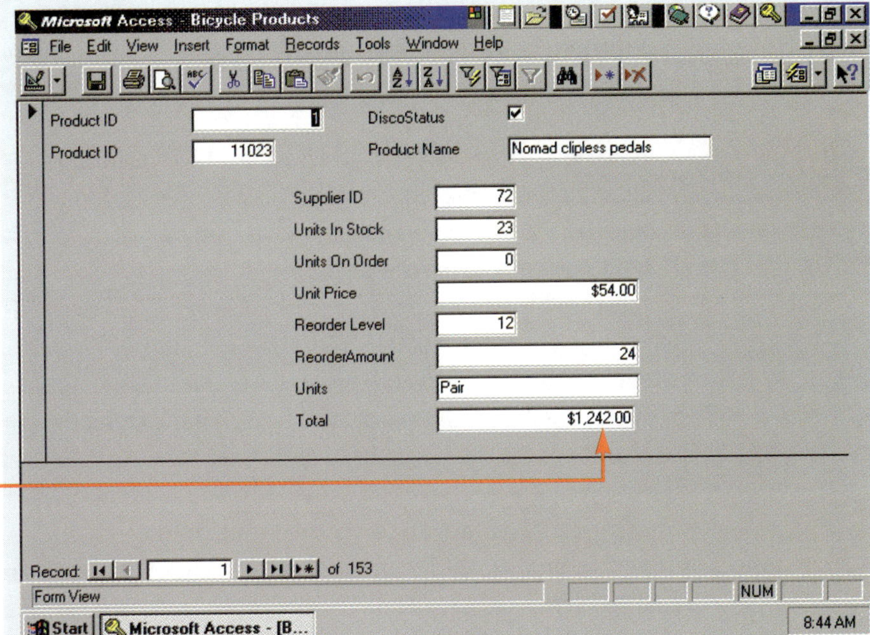

Aligning controls

In Design View, you can align controls with other controls. First, you must select the controls you want to align by pressing [Shift] while clicking the controls. After selecting all the necessary controls, click Format on the menu bar, click Align, then click the alignment position you want, as shown in Figure 4-15.

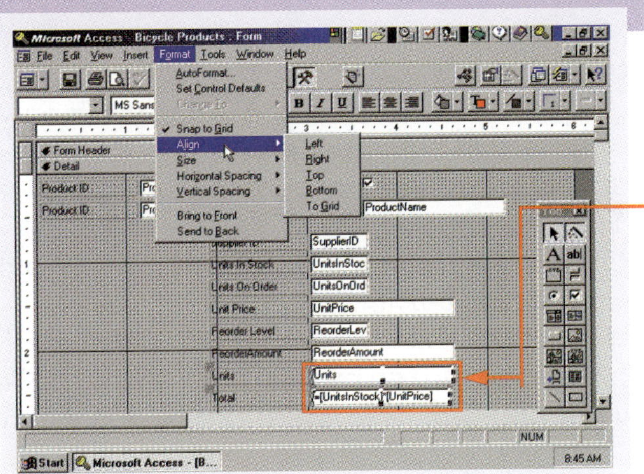

Selected controls

FIGURE 4-15: Aligning controls

QUICK **TIP**

You can delete a control by selecting it with the mouse, then pressing [Delete].■

Using a form to add a record

After you create a form, you can use it to add records to the database table. To add a record you press [Tab] to move from field to field, entering the appropriate information. You can also print a form to obtain a hard copy for sharing with others. ▶**case** Michael will use the Bicycle Products form to add a new record to the Bicycle Products table. Then he'll print the form with the data for the new record, and distribute the form to other Nomad employees so that they can see how to use the form to enter data. Because the Bicycle Products table is already selected in the Database window, Michael begins by opening the form.

1 Click the **Open button** in the Database window
Michael maximizes the form to make it easier to see all the fields.

2 Click the **Maximize button** if necessary to maximize the form
Now Michael can add the new record.

3 Click the **New Record button** ▶* on the Form View toolbar
A new, blank record is displayed. The text "(AutoNumber)" appears in the first Product ID field. (Recall that the first Product ID field is the Counter field for the table; the second Product ID field contains the actual product identification numbers for the items in the bicycle inventory.) Record 154 of 154 appears in the status bar. See Figure 4-16. Michael begins to enter the data for the new record.

4 Press **[Tab]** to advance to the next field
The cursor moves to the DiscoStatus field. Remember that when you created the form, you changed the tab order so that DiscoStatus would be the second field moved to in the form. Michael will leave the DiscoStatus field blank to indicate that the product is currently offered (he would enter a checkmark in this field for a product that is discontinued). Michael continues to enter the data for the record, pressing [Tab] to move from field to field.

5 Press **[Tab]** to advance to the second Product ID field, type **57129**, press **[Tab]**, type **Nomad FinneganFast Tire**, press **[Tab]**, type **22**, press **[Tab]**, type **14**, press **[Tab]**, type **20**, press **[Tab]**, type **15.50**, press **[Tab]**, type **15**, press **[Tab]**, type **20**, press **[Tab]**, type **Each**, then press **[Enter]**
Compare your completed record to Figure 4-17. Notice that the Total field shows the calculated result. The new record is stored in the Bicycle Products table. Next Michael wants to print the form containing the new record.

6 Click the **Print Preview button** 🔍 on the Form View toolbar, then click the **Last Record button** ▶❙
The status bar indicates that the last record, the one Michael just added, is on page 50. Michael wants to print only this page.

7 Click **File** on the menu bar, click **Print**, type **49** in the From text box, type **50** in the To text box, then click **OK**
Michael closes the Print Preview window, then closes the form and returns to the Database window.

8 Click the **Close button** on the Print Preview toolbar, click **File** on the menu bar, click **Close**, then click **Yes** to save the changes

FIGURE 4-16: Blank form for new record

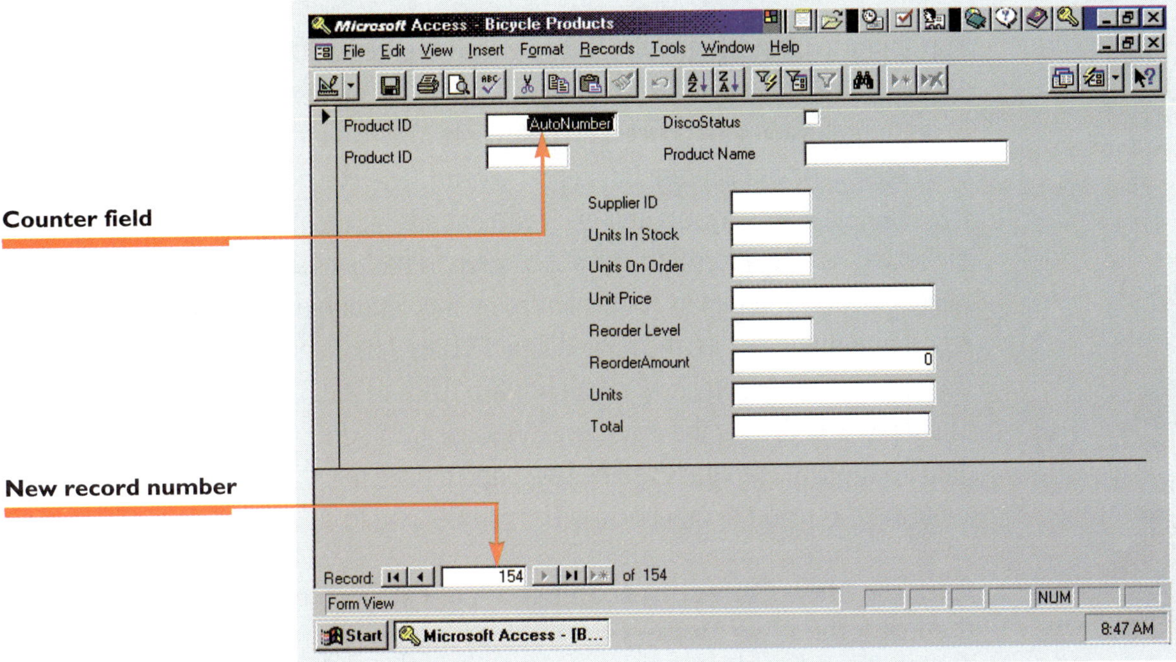

FIGURE 4-17: Completed record 154

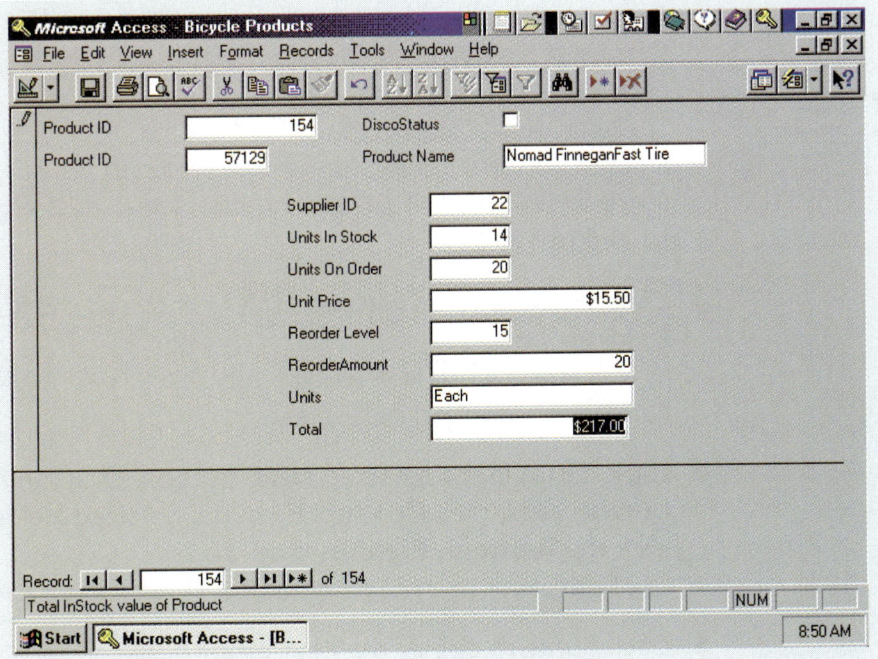

Creating a report

The ability to create thoughtful, concise reports enables you to share data with others in meaningful ways. The most significant data can lose its impact if it appears in an unprofessional or poorly laid out report. You can create reports in Access from scratch or you can use the Report Wizard. The **Report Wizard** provides sample report layouts and gives you options for including specific fields in the report. As with a form, the layout of a report includes sections for a Report Header, Detail, and Report Footer. For more information on creating a simple report automatically, see the related topic "Using AutoReport." **case** Michael wants to create a report showing all but two fields in the Bicycle Products table. The report will display the inventory in groups by product name so that all of the data for the same products will be listed and totaled together. Michael plans on distributing this report to other Nomad employees and to customers.

1 Click the **New Object button list arrow** 🗐 on the Database toolbar, then click the **New Report** from the palette
The New Report dialog box opens. You could also create a report by clicking the Report object button in the Database window, then clicking New. Michael uses the Bicycle Products table for his report, which he'll create using the Report Wizard.

2 Click the **Choose the table or query where the object's data comes from list arrow**, click **Bicycle Products**, click **Report Wizard**, then click **OK**
The Report Wizard dialog box opens. This dialog box allows you to select which fields appear in the report. Michael wants all fields except the Product ID and Total fields to be included. Rather than individually select all but these two fields, Michael selects all the fields and then deletes the two he doesn't want.

3 Click the **All Fields button** 🔲 to move all the fields to the Selected Fields list box
All fields in the Available fields list move to the Selected Fields list. Now Michael can remove the fields he doesn't want included in the report.

4 Click **Total** in the Selected Fields list box, click the **Remove Field button** 🔲, click **ProductID** in the Selected Fields list box, then click the **Remove Field button** 🔲
Your Field order on report list box should look like the one in Figure 4-18.

5 Click **Next** to display the next dialog box
This dialog box, shown in Figure 4-19, determines how the data in the report will be grouped. Continue with the next lesson to finish creating the report.

FIGURE 4-18: Completed field order list box

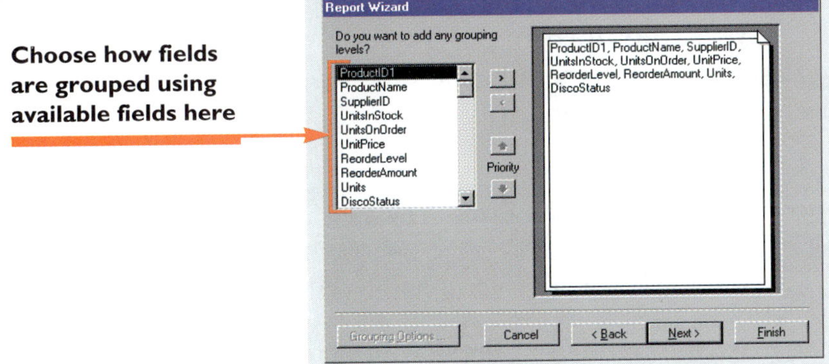

Remaining available fields appear here

Fields in report appear here

FIGURE 4-19: Grouping dialog box

Choose how fields are grouped using available fields here

Using AutoReport

You can create a simple report quickly by selecting the New Object button on the Database toolbar, then selecting AutoReport on the palette. AutoReport offers no prompts or dialog boxes; it instantly creates a single-column report that displays all fields in the table or query.

Creating a report, continued

Michael wants the records grouped by product name so that all the same products will appear together in the report.

7 Click **ProductName**, click the **Single Field button** [›], then click **Next**

This dialog box allows you to specify a sort order. Michael chooses to sort by DiscoStatus so that the report will show all current items together and all discontinued items together.

8 Click the **first list arrow**, then click **DiscoStatus**

Next, Michael chooses which items will be totalled.

9 Click **Summary Options**, add a checkmark to each item in the Sum column, click **OK**, then click **Next**

The following two dialog boxes ask you to select a report style, paper orientation, and report title. Michael accepts the default choices.

10 Click the **Landscape radio button**, click **Next**, click **Next** again, type **Products by DiscoStatus** in the title text box, then click **Finish**

Access compiles the report. The report is saved as part of the database file. Michael wants to preview the report.

11 Click the **Zoom button** 🔍 on the Print Preview toolbar

The report appears, as shown in Figure 4-20. Notice that the records are grouped by product name. Michael is satisfied with the report and needs to save his work.

12 Click the **Close button** on the Print Preview toolbar

Michael decides to print just the first page of the report to see how it looks.

13 Click **File** on the menu bar, click **Print**, type **1** in the From text box, type **1** in the To text box, then click **OK**

Compare your printout to Figure 4-21.

FIGURE 4-20: Previewing the report

Records grouped by Product Name

Pointer changes to Magnifier pointer

FIGURE 4-21: Printed report

Products by DiscoStatus

ProductName	DiscoStat	roduct ID	upplier ID	nits In Stock	its On Order	nit Price	order Level	orderAmount	Units
Look PP166 pedals									
	☑	11162	63	45	0	$45.00	10	36	Pair
	☑	11162	63	45	0	$45.00	10	36	Pair
	☐	11162	63	45	0	$45.75	10	36	Pair
	☐	11162	94	45	0	$45.00	10	36	Pair
	☐	11162	63	45	0	$45.00	10	36	Pair
	☐	11162	91	45	0	$45.00	10	36	Pair
	☐	11162	63	45	0	$45.00	10	36	Pair
Summary for 'ProductName' = Look PP166 pedals (7 detail records)									
Sum	Yes	78134	500	315	0	315.75	70	252	
Look PP166 pedals - ad									
	☐	11162	63	45	0	$45.00	10	36	Pair
Summary for 'ProductName' = Look PP166 pedals - adv (1 detail record)									
Sum	No	11162	63	45	0	45	10	36	
Look PP168 pedals									
	☐	11162	63	45	0	$45.00	10	36	Pair
Summary for 'ProductName' = Look PP168 pedals (1 detail record)									
Sum	No	11162	63	45	0	45	10	36	
Nomad Aerospoke Whee									
	☑	76662	56	30	0	$200.00	15	30	Each
	☑	76662	52	30	0	$200.00	15	30	Each
	☑	76662	51	30	0	$200.00	15	30	Each

Friday, October 20, 1995

Page 1 of 11

Modifying a report

You can make modifications to the format of a report, such as bolding column headings or changing the alignment of fields in a column. The Report Design window is divided into seven sections—**Detail**, which contains controls and the compiled data from the table, and a Header and Footer section for each of the following: Report, Page, and Group. The **Group Header** references the field on which each group is based (in this case, the groups are based on Product Name). The **Report Header** and **Report Footer** print only on the first and last page of the report; the Page Header and Page Footer print on every page. ▶case Although the Products by DiscoStatus report is adequate, Michael wants to give the report a more professional look. The field headings are not aligned with the data below them, as shown in Figure 4-22. Because Michael's screen is already in Design View, he can easily align the field headings with their data to format the report. Michael uses [Shift] to select multiple controls for aligning.

1 Press and hold **[Shift]** while selecting each of the control headings in the Page Header section, *except* Product Name
While pressing and holding [Shift] and selecting controls, you might need to scroll the window to select all the desired controls. Each selected control has handles surrounding it. First Michael centers the selected controls and decreases the font size to make the text less crowded.

2 Click the **Center button** 🔳 on the Report Design toolbar, click the **Font Size list arrow**, then click **8**
Access centers the headings for the selected controls in the Page Header section. See Figure 4-23. Michael wants to center align the controls in the Detail section of the report.

3 Select the **ProductID1** control in the Detail section
Selecting this control without holding [Shift] deselects the previously selected controls. Michael continues to make multiple selections in the Detail section.

4 Press and hold **[Shift]** while selecting each of the control headings in the Detail section, then click 🔳 on the Report Design toolbar
Access centers the headings for the selected controls in the Detail section. Michael decides that the information in the ProductName Footer section is unnecessary and wants to delete it, but first deselects the controls in the Detail section.

5 Select the first control in the ProductName footer section

6 Press **[Shift]** while selecting each of the controls in the ProductName Footer section, then press **[Delete]**
The report now has a gap in it created by the deleted controls. Michael will close the gap by changing the row width using the Page Footer divider. The Page Footer divider is the top of the bar containing the section name "Page Footer." He can drag the divider up to narrow the gap.

7 Drag the **Page Footer divider** up toward the ProductName Footer section as shown in Figure 4-24
You might have to move the Toolbox toolbar in order to see the ruler.
Continue with the next lesson to finish modifying the report.

FIGURE 4-22:
Unedited Products by
DiscoStatus report

Headings and data are
not aligned

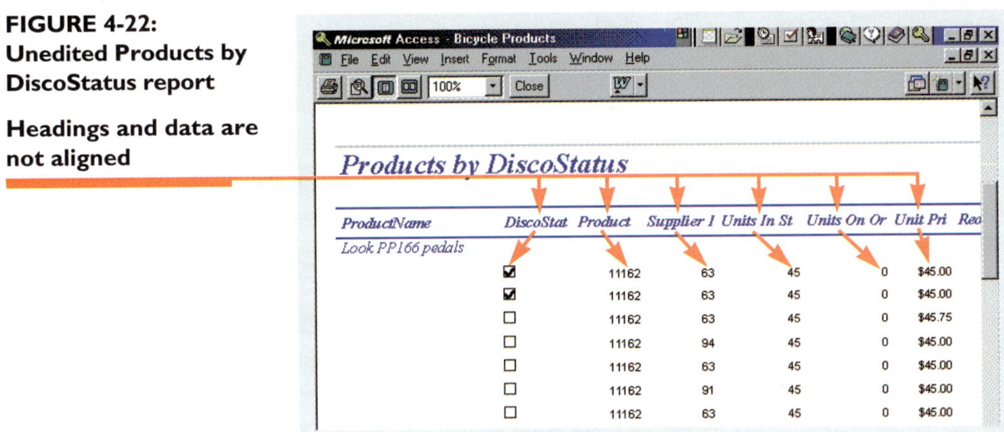

FIGURE 4-23:
Centered controls in
the report

Center button
indented

Selected controls

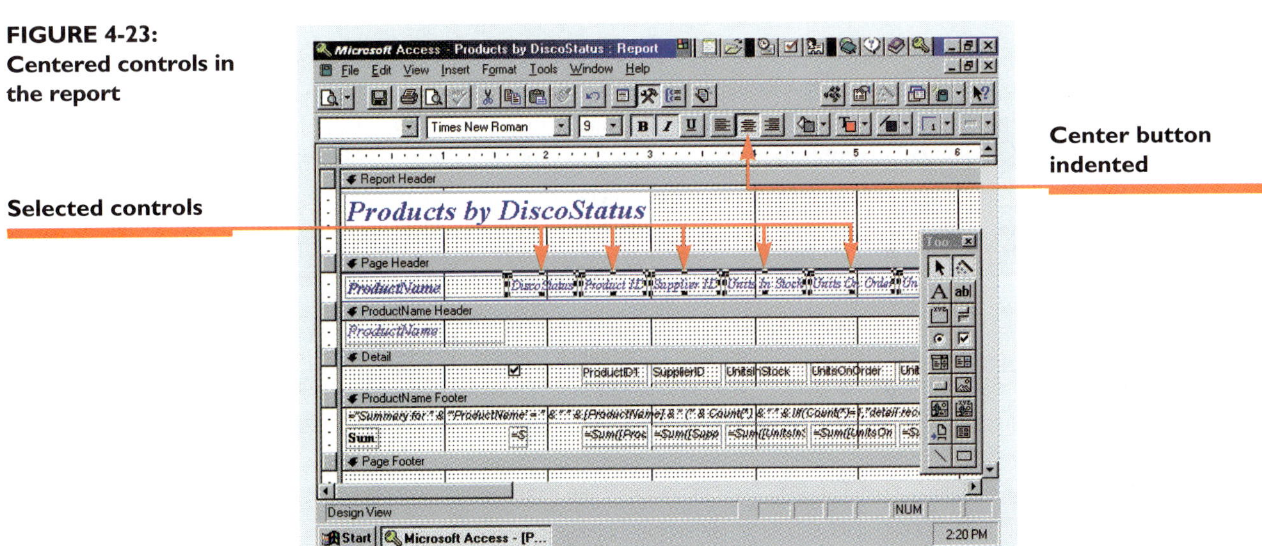

FIGURE 4-24: Narrowing the width between sections

Resizing pointer

Page Footer divider

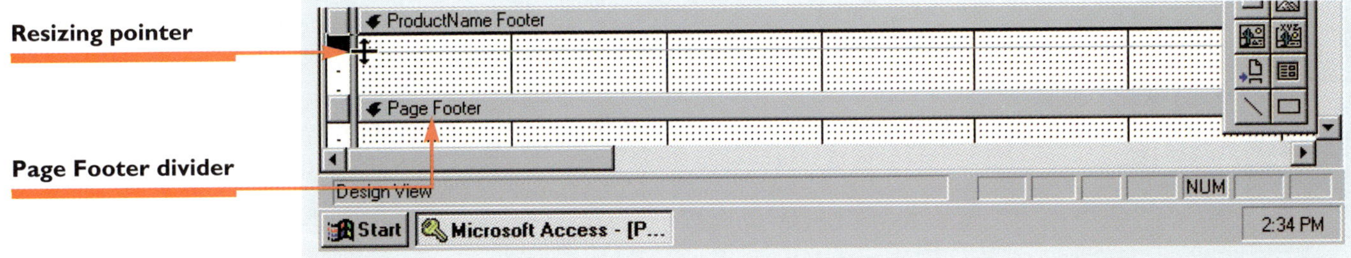

Modifying a report, continued

Next Michael needs to resize the Detail control widths so that they match the Page Header controls. ▶ Also, for information on saving a form as a report, see the related topic "Saving a form as a report" on the next page.

8 Click the **ProductID1** control in the Detail section, move the pointer to the right middle handle until the pointer changes to ↔, then drag the handle until it is aligned with the width of the ProductID control in the Page Header section, as shown in Figure 4-25
This process must be repeated for the remaining controls in the Detail section.

9 Repeat Step 8 to resize the SupplierID, UnitsInStock, UnitsOnOrder, UnitPrice, ReorderAmount, Units, and DiscoStatus controls in the Detail section with their corresponding controls in the Page Header section
Each of the controls in the Detail section is now aligned and resized with its control in the Header section. Michael wants to preview the report and print a sample page of the report.

10 Click the **Print Preview button** on the Report Design toolbar
The controls in the report are aligned, as shown in Figure 4-26.

11 Click **File** on the menu bar, click **Print**, click **1** in the From text box, click **1** in the To text box, then click **OK**
Michael closes the Print Preview window and saves the report.

12 Click the **Close button** on the Print Preview toolbar, then click the **Save button** on the Report Design toolbar

FIGURE 4-25: Resizing a control

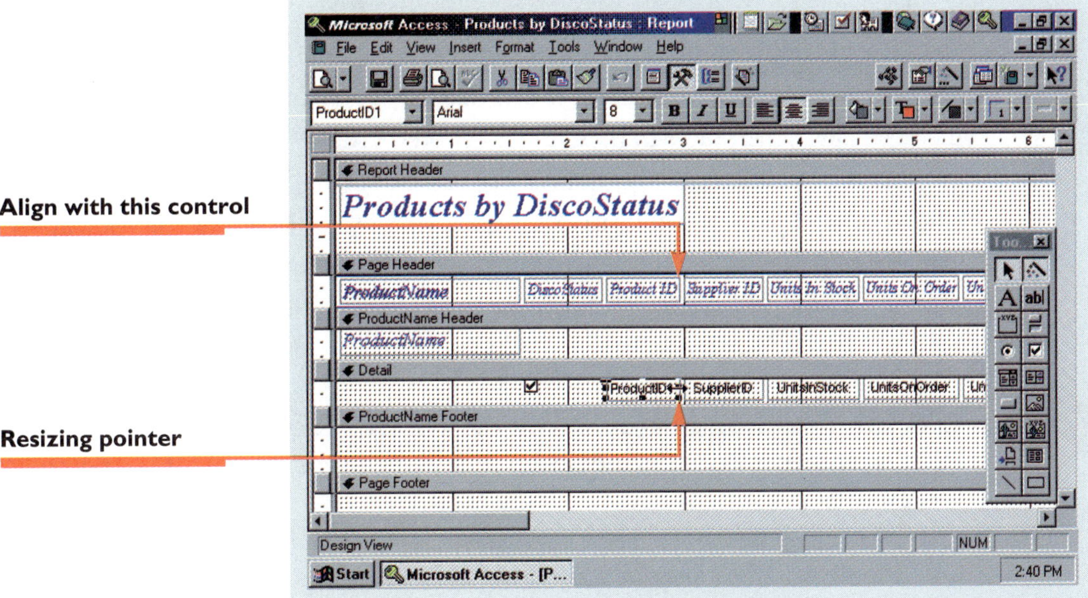

Align with this control

Resizing pointer

FIGURE 4-26: Report in Print Preview

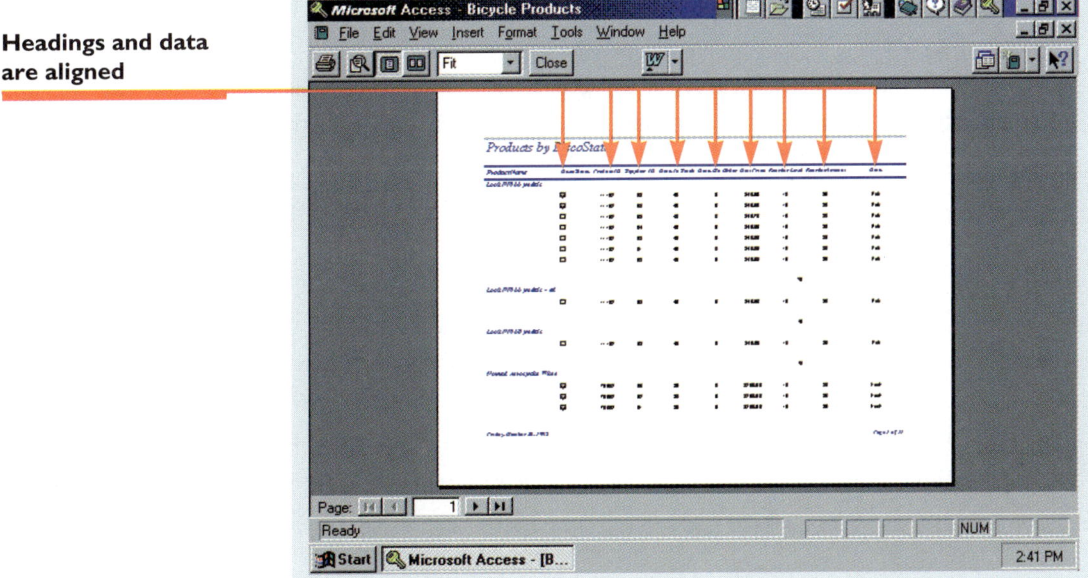

Headings and data
are aligned

Saving a form as a report

You can save a form as a report, which saves you the time and effort of having to
recreate an existing format. To save a form as a report, open the form in Design
View, click File on the menu bar, click Save As Report, then supply a new name for
the report.

Adding an expression to a report

You have already seen how an expression can be incorporated in a form. You can also add an expression to a report to perform calculations. The expression can include field names, table names, and functions. A function is an easy-to-use pre-programmed mathematical equation. For more information on functions, see the related topic "Using functions in expressions." **case** Michael wants to add an expression to the Products by DiscoStatus report. The expression will count the number of products in each group, by product identification number.

1 Click the **Text box button** ▭ on the Toolbox toolbar, then click in the **ProductName Footer section** directly under the ProductID1 control at the 2¼" mark
This places an unbound control in the ProductName Footer section, into which Michael will type the expression. The expression will include the Count function, which counts the number of occurrences of a specified field in a column.

2 Click inside the unbound control, type **=Count([ProductID1])**, then press **[Enter]**
The expression appears in the control, as shown in Figure 4-27, although some of its contents might be truncated, or cut off. Michael wants to preview the report to see the results of the expression.

3 Click the **Print Preview button** ▭ on the Report Design toolbar
The number of records in each group has been counted, although the values need to be aligned with the values in the ProductID1 column.

4 Click the **Close button** on the Print Preview toolbar, then click the **Left-Align button** ▭ on the Report Design toolbar
Michael decides to preview the report again to check the results of this modification.

5 Click ▭, view the results of the modified control, then click the **Close button**
As shown in Print Preview, the value in the expression is left-aligned in the Product ID column. Michael needs to add a label to describe what the values represent in the report.

6 Click the text box to the left of the expression, select the text in the box, type **Items in Category:**, press **[Enter]**, click the **Font Size list arrow**, click **9**
The label is added to the report as shown in Figure 4-28. Michael again previews his report.

7 Click ▭
Compare your previewed report with Figure 4-29. Michael prints the first page of the report, then closes the Print Preview window and saves his modifications.

8 Click **File** on the menu bar, click **Print**, type **1** in the From text box, type **1** in the To text box, click **OK**, click the **Close button** on the Print Preview toolbar, then click the **Save button** ▭ on the Report Design toolbar

9 Click **File** on the menu bar, then click **Close**

FIGURE 4-27: Truncated expression in control

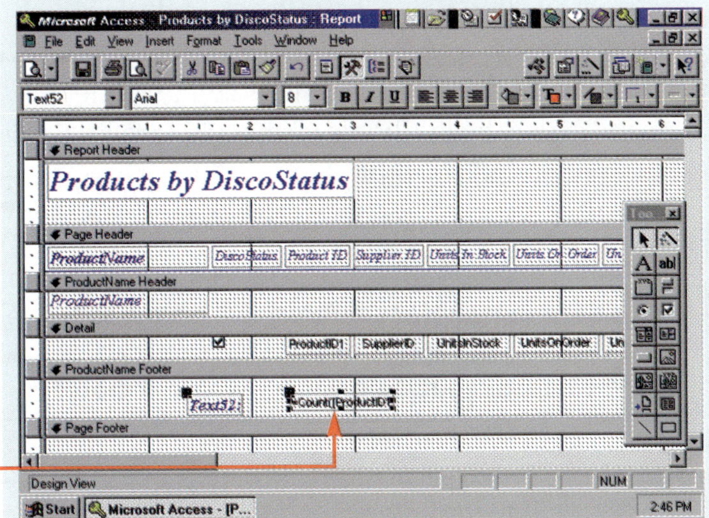

Expression indicating
Count function

FIGURE 4-28: Descriptive label added to expression

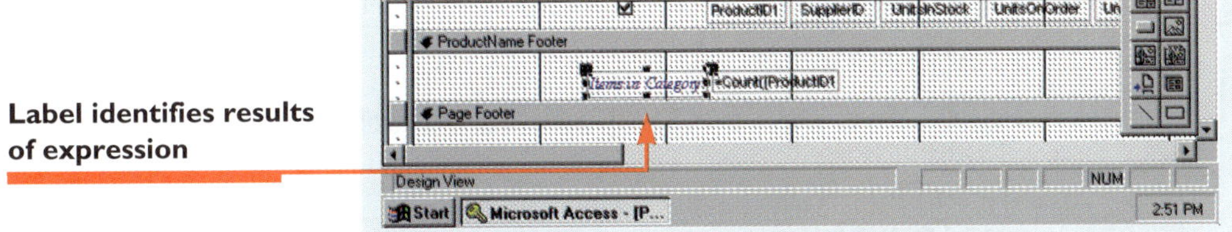

Label identifies results
of expression

FIGURE 4-29: Completed report with expression and label

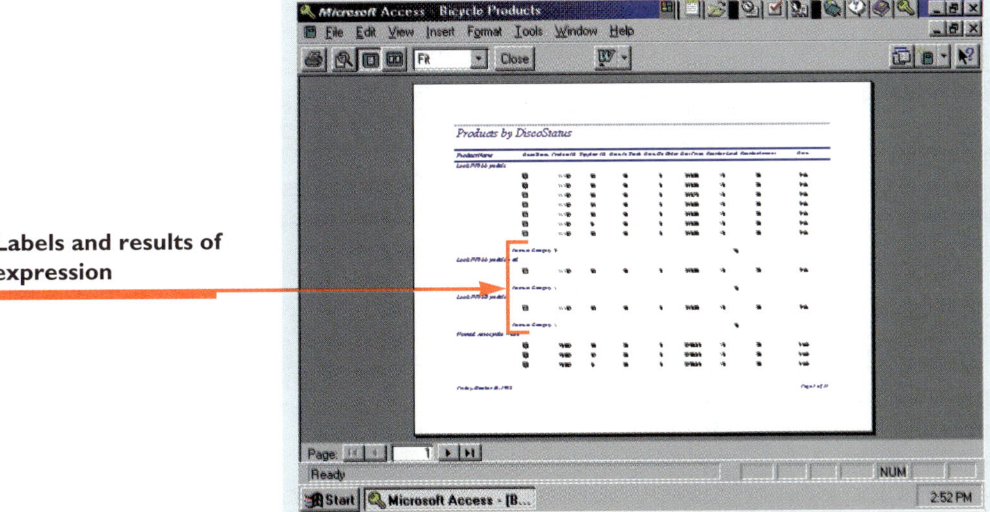

Labels and results of
expression

Using functions in expressions

In addition to Count, Access provides many other functions for use in expressions.
Using Access Help, you can search for the topic "Functions" to display a list of
available functions and how to use them.

Creating a report from a query

You've seen how to create a report based on the fields in a table. Many times, however, you will want to use a query as the basis for a report. **case** Michael has created a query for the Bicycle Products table called Current Product List to display only current products. He wants to use this query as the basis for a new report. Again, he'll use the Report Wizard to create this report.

1. Click the **New Object button list arrow** on the Database toolbar, then click the **New Report** on the palette, click **Current Product List** in the Choose the table or query where the object's data comes from list box, click **Report Wizard**, then click **OK**

   The Report Wizard dialog box opens, as shown in Figure 4-30. The Available fields list box displays all the fields used in the query (not all the fields in the table). Michael wants to include all the fields in the report.

2. Click the **All Fields button**, then click **Next**

   Michael wants the records sorted by ProductName. The next two dialog boxes contain default settings for the report's appearance, paper orientation, and title, which Michael accepts.

3. Click **ProductName**, click the **Single Field button**, click **Next**, then click **Finish**

   Access creates the report and displays it in Print Preview. Michael needs to make a few minor modifications to the alignment of controls.

4. Click the **Close button** on the Print Preview toolbar

   Michael wants to center the headings for Product ID, Supplier ID, Units In Stock, and Unit Price. He does this by selecting these controls and then using the Center button.

5. In the PageHeader section click the **ProductID control**, press and hold **[Shift]**, click the controls for **SupplierID**, **UnitsInStock**, and **UnitPrice**, then click the **Center button** on the Report Design toolbar

   Access centers the headings for the selected controls in the Page Header section. Michael wants to center align the controls in the Detail section of the report.

6. In the Detail section click the **ProductID1 control**, press and hold **[Shift]** while clicking the **SupplierID**, **UnitsInStock**, and **UnitPrice** controls then click

   Michael previews and prints the report to see his modifications.

7. Click the **Print Preview button** on the Report Design toolbar, click the **Print button** on the Print Preview toolbar

   Compare page 1 of your printed report with Figure 4-31. Michael closes the Print Preview window, saves his modifications, and closes the report.

8. Click the **Close Button** on the Print Preview toolbar, click the **Save button** on the Report Design toolbar, click **File** on the menu bar, then click **Exit**

FIGURE 4-30: Report Wizard dialog box

Fields available in query

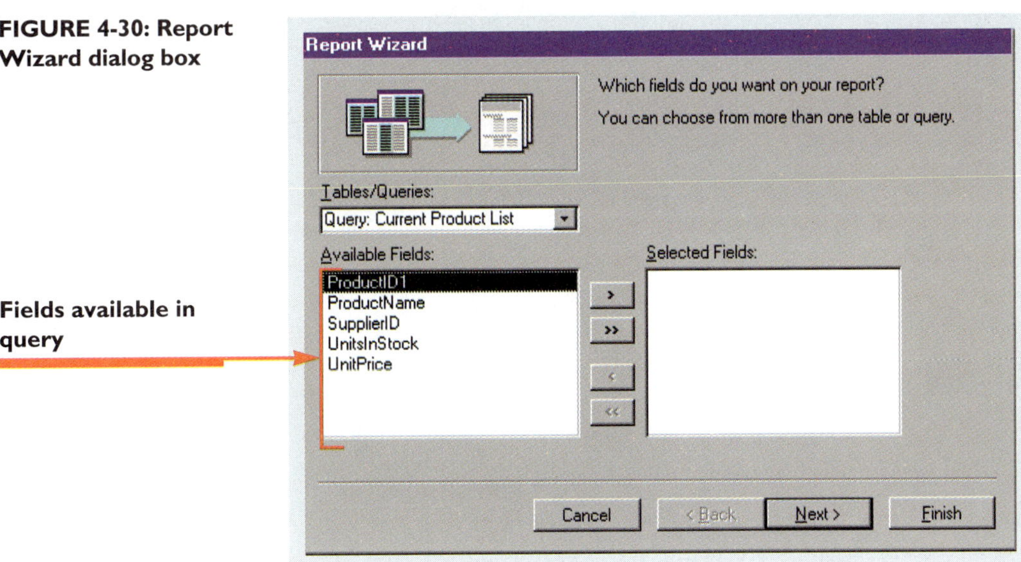

FIGURE 4-31: Completed report created from a query

Current Product List

ProductName	Product ID	Supplier ID	Units In Stock	Unit Price
Look PP166 pedals				
	11162	63	45	$45.75
	11162	94	45	$45.00
	11162	91	45	$45.00
	11162	63	45	$45.00
	11162	63	45	$45.00
Look PP166 pedals - adv				
	11162	63	45	$45.00
Look PP168 pedals				
	11162	63	45	$45.00
Nomad Aerospoke Wheels				
	76662	56	30	$200.00
	76662	56	30	$200.00
	76662	56	30	$200.00
	76662	56	30	$200.00
Nomad Aerospoke Wheels - Pr				
	76662	56	30	$200.00
Nomad Beauty Handlebar tap				
	32323	10	27	$3.00
	32323	10	27	$2.00
Nomad clipless pedals				
	11023	54	20	$54.50
	11023	72	23	$54.00
	11023	.'2	23	$54.00
	11023	72	23	$54.00
	11023	72	23	$54.00
	11023	72	23	$54.00
Nomad FinneganFast Tire				
	57129	22	14	$15.50
Nomad Nicole Handlebar tape				
	32323	10	27	$2.00

Friday, October 20, 1995   *Page 1 of 4*

QUICK **TIP**

When basing a report on a query, give the report the same name as the query name; this will remind you that the report and the query are related.

TASKREFERENCE

TASK	MOUSE/BUTTON	MENU	KEYBOARD
Add a record from Form View		Click Insert, Record	[Alt] [I], [R]
Add a single field			
Add all fields			
Add an Expression to a report	, then type the expression		
Align selected controls		Click Format, Align, then Left, Right, Top, Bottom, or To Grid	[Alt] [O], [L], ([L], [R], [T], [B], or [G])
Build an Expression	Click Data tab,		
Change the Tab Order		Click View, Tab Order	[Alt] [V], [E]
Create a new Form	Click the Forms tab from the Database window, then click New	Click Insert, Form	[Alt] [I], [F]
Create a new Report from a table or query	Click the Reports tab in the database window, then click New	Click Insert, Report	[Alt] [I], [R]
Create an AutoForm	, then click AutoForm		
Create an AutoReport	, then click AutoReport		
Delete a selected control		Click Edit, Delete	[Del]
Open Properties Sheet		Click View, Properties	[Alt] [V], [P]
Remove a single field			
Remove all fields			
Select a control	Click control		
Select multiple controls	Click controls while holding [Shift]		
Switch to Design View		Click View, Form Design	[Alt] [V], [D]
Switch to Form View		Click View, Form	[Alt] [V], [F]

CONCEPTS REVIEW

Label each of the elements of the Report Design window shown in Figure 4-32.

1

2

3

4

5

6

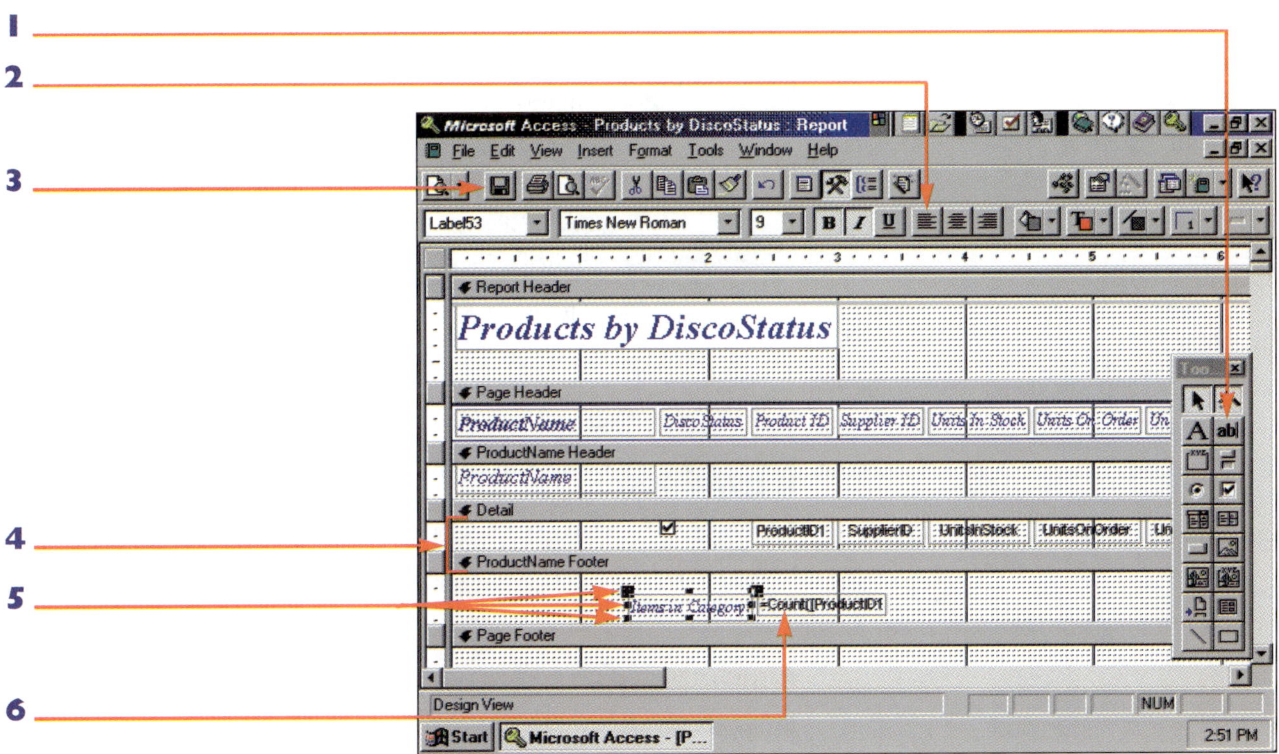

FIGURE 4-32

Match each button to its correct description.

7

8 New Report

9

10

11

12

a. Print Preview

b. Zoom

c. New Object

d. Form View

e. Design View

f. New Report

Select the best answer from the list of choices.

13 Objects in a form or report are called

  a. Properties

  b. Controls

  c. Pieces

  d. Handles

14 The pointer used to resize a control is

  a.

  b.

  c.

  d.

15 A control is considered to be bound when

  a. It is displayed in a form or report

  b. It is used to sort a table

  c. Its data source is found in a table

  d. Its data source is the result of an expression

SKILLSREVIEW

1 Create a form.

a. Start Access and make sure your Student Disk is in drive A. Open the file Bike Parts from your Student Disk.

b. Create a new form for the Products table.

c. Include all fields in the form.

d. Use the Form Wizard to create a columnar form.

e. Use the Stone style.

f. Use the title Bicycle Parts Database for the form.

g. Display the form with data.

2 Modify a form.

a. Maximize the Form window and change the form's dimensions so that it is at least 6" wide.

b. Select controls and position them so that all controls are displayed on the screen in an order you feel makes sense.

c. Modify the tab order so that pressing [Tab] moves sequentially through the fields as you have arranged them.

d. Write down your new tab order, and turn the list in.

3 Modify controls.

a. Change the format of the UnitsOnOrder control so that it has one decimal place.

b. Change the number contained in the UnitsInStock field so that it appears in italics.

c. View the changes in Form View.

d. Save your changes.

4 Add a record using a form.

a. Open the Product Entry Form.

b. Enter the following new record: Product ID: 70701, Product Name: Nomad Honey Handlebar tape, Category ID: 32, Supplier ID: 10, Units In Stock: 52, Units On Order: 0, Unit Price: 2, Reorder Level: 30, Reorder Amount: 35, Units: Each, DiscoStatus: No.

c. Save the record.

d. Print the form containing the new record.

5 Create a report.

a. Create a Groups/Totals report based on the Products sold as "Each" query using the table Report Wizard.

b. Include all the fields in the report.

c. Group the report by Units in Stock

d. Sort the report by Product Name.

e. Preview the report with the data in it.

f. Print the report.

g. Save the report as Products by Units in Stock.

6 Modify a report.

a. Align the fields so that the values are centered with the headings above them.

b. Delete any calculated summaries you feel detract from the report.

c. Preview and print the report.

d. Save your changes.

7 Add an expression to a report.

a. Create an expression in the Detail section under Product Name that subtracts Reorder Level from Units in Stock.

b. Add the descriptive label "Reorder if Negative" to the left of the expression.

c. Preview and print the report.

d. Save your changes.

INDEPENDENT CHALLENGE 1

As the Customer Service Manager of the Melodies Music Store, you must continue your work on the music database. Several of the store's employees will be using the database to enter data, and you need to design a form to facilitate this data entry. The employees will be entering data from a paper-based form, shown in Figure 4-33. You also need to generate reports for output requests by management as well as customers.

FIGURE 4-33

To complete this independent challenge:

1 Open the file Melodies Music Database from your Student Disk.

2 Create a single-column form that includes all the fields in the table, then save it as Title Input.

3 The controls should be positioned so that they all fit on the screen. Make sure the tab order reflects any fields that you moved.

4 Use the newly created form to add three new records of your favorite artists.

5 Print the form containing one of the new records.

6 Add an expression that calculates a new field called OnHand that multiplies the UnitsInStock field value by the UnitPrice field value.

7 Create a report based on the Available titles table query, which displays all fields in a Groups/Totals format.

8 Save the report as Music Titles then print the report.

INDEPENDENT
CHALLENGE 2

You work in the U.S. Census Office for your city. The records in the Statistical Data table, which is in the database file US Census Statistics on your Student Disk, contain marriage information by state. Each state is assigned a geographical area. Using the Statistical Data table, create a form to facilitate data entry, and create at least two reports showing different groupings of this information.

To complete this independent challenge:

1 Create a single-column form containing all the fields in the table.

2 Modify the form by repositioning the controls, then adjusting the tab order.

3 Save the form using a name of your choice.

4 Preview the form after each of your modifications.

5 Create at least two forms based on information in the table. Save each form using a name of your choice. Try saving each form as a report.

6 Print a sample of each report.

7 Create reports of your choosing based on each of the queries saved in the US Census Statistics database file. Each report should show all the fields in each query, and use a format you feel best shows the data.

8 Print the reports.

INDEPENDENT
CHALLENGE 3

The medical consortium, Allied Surgeons and Physicians, would like to customize their new database to enhance its effectiveness and efficiency. Using the Allied Surgeons and Physicians database on your Student Disk, create forms and reports that will make it easy for patient entries to be made.

To complete this independent challenge:

1 Create a form using the Patient Records table which displays all the fields in the table.

2 Arrange the fields in a way that seems efficient for data entry.

3 Make sure the tab order is updated to reflect the new order of fields.

4 Use the new form to add one new patient for each physician.

5 Print the form containing your new entries.

6 Add an expression that calculates each patient's current age.

7 Create a report based on each Physician's Patient List.

8 Submit all printouts.

VISUALWORKSHOP

Use the Current Product List query in the Bike Inventory database on your Student Disk to create the following form using the skills you learned in this Unit.

FIGURE 4-34

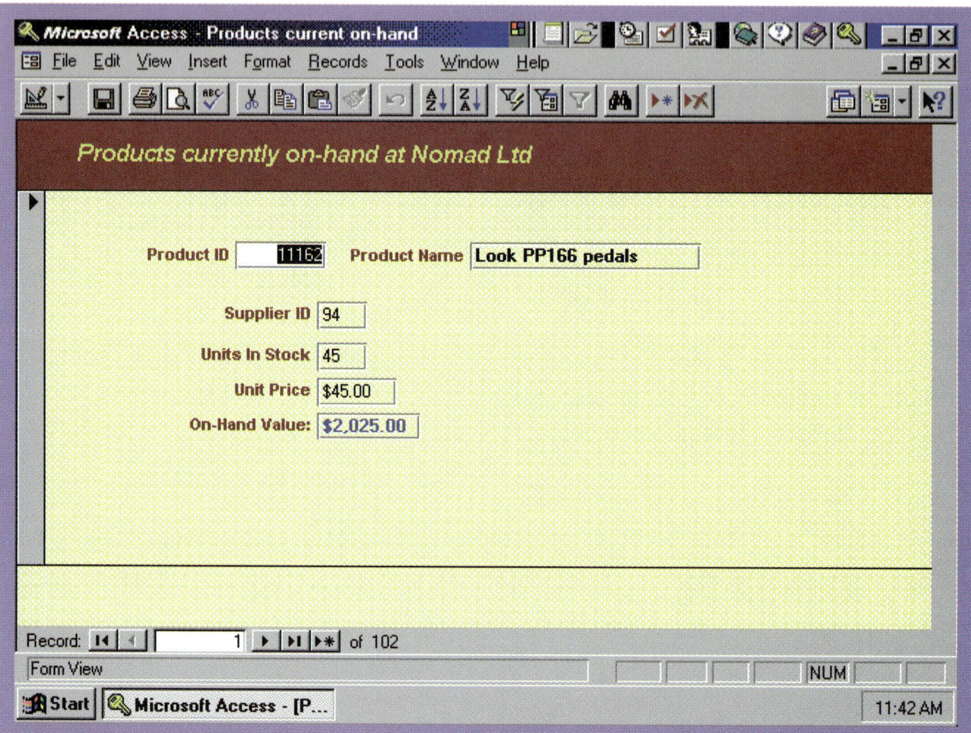

Glossary

AND and OR criteria   Parameters used to qualify records selected in a query or filter. AND is used to narrow the number of selected records, whereas OR is used to broaden the number of selected records.

Ascending order   A sort order in which fields are alphabetized from A to Z.

AutoReport   Button that automatically creates a report that displays all fields in a single-column format.

Bound control   A control on a form that is linked to a specific field in the database. *See also* Control.

Calculated control   A control that has a mathematical expression as its data source.

Cell   The intersection of a column and a row.

Control   A graphical object that consists of the field text and the data in it. Controls are either bound, unbound, or calculated.

Counter field   A field that automatically assigns the next consecutive number each time a record is added.

Data   The information contained in a database table.

Database   A collection of data related to a particular topic or purpose.

Database window   The window that opens when you start Access. It provides access to the objects in the database.

Datasheet   A grid in which each record is contained in a row, and field names are listed as column headings. You enter data for a table in the datasheet.

Datasheet View   A window that displays records in a grid format of columns and rows, which you can use to navigate through the records quickly.

Descending order   A sort order in which fields are alphabetized from Z to A.

Design View   A window that shows the structure of a table, form, query, or report. You use this view to modify the structure of a table by adding and deleting fields and adding field descriptions and field properties.

Detail   Section of a form that appears on the screen form and displays the fields and data for each record visible in Design View. Detail section also appears in Report Design window, in which you can make modifications to the format of a report.

Dynaset   Collection of records resulting from a query; looks and acts like a table, but is merely a view based on the query.

Expression   A mathematical equation created within a form or report's control.

Expression Builder   A feature that displays helpful fields and mathematical symbols you use to create expressions.

Field   Category of information in a database table, such as a customer's last name.

Field description   Optional text that clarifies the purpose or function of a field. The field description appears in the status bar when you enter data.

Field properties   Information you can define that affects the data entered in a field, such as the number of decimal places in a number. You define field properties in the Design view.

Filter window   A window that consists of two areas: the field list on top, containing all the fields in the table, and the filter grid on the bottom, into which fields are dragged and filtering criteria are defined.

Filtering   A more complex method of organizing records, in which you define the fields on which the table is sorted.

Form   An object used to enter, edit, and display records one at a time.

Form Footer   A section of a form that appears at the bottom of each screen form and can contain totals, instructions, or command buttons.

Form Header   A section of a form that appears at the beginning of each screen form and can contain a title or logo.

Form View   Screen in which table data can be viewed, entered, or changed one record at a time.

Form Wizard   A feature that guides you through the process of creating a form by providing sample form layouts and form-specific options.

Function   An easy-to-use preprogrammed mathematical equation that can be used in forms and reports to make calculations.

Handles   Black squares that appear around the perimeter of a control, indicating the control is selected.

Help   On-line system that gives you immediate access to definitions, explanations, and useful tips as they related to Access.

Input   Materials necessary to produce the results you want.

Mouse pointer   An arrow indicating the location of the mouse on the desktop. The mouse pointer changes shape at times, depending on the application and task being executed or performed.

Object   The principal component of an Access database. Tables, queries, forms, and reports are all referred to as objects in Access.

Object buttons   Buttons on the left side of the database window that allow you to open, create, and modify database components.

Output   The desired results of a database, often printed reports or screen forms.

Page Footer   Material that appears at the bottom of each page in printed output.

Page Header   Material that appears at the top of each page in printed output.

Primary key   A field that qualifies each record as unique. If you do not specify a primary key, Access will create one for you.

Print Preview   A window that displays a view of how a page will appear when printed.

Property   Quality or characteristic of a control that makes data entry more efficient.

Property Sheet   A window that displays the control's name and source and that lists the qualities for the selected control that can be edited.

Query   A set of qualities, or criteria, that you specify to retrieve certain data from a database. You can save a query to use at a later time.

Query grid   Area in which fields and query instructions are contained.

Record   A group of related fields, such as all information on a particular customer.

Relational database   A database that contains more than one table and allows information within its tables to be shared.

Report   An Access object that presents data selected and formatted for printing.

Report Footer   Material that appears at the bottom of the last printed page of a report.

Report Header   Material that appears at the top of the first printed page of a report.

Report Wizard   A feature that guides you through the process of creating a report by providing sample report layouts and options for including specific fields in the report.

Row selector   A gray box at the left edge of a datasheet that is used to select an entire row.

Select query   A query that created a dynaset in which records are collected and viewed, and can be modified.

Shortcut keys   A key or key combination that allows you to select a command without using the menu bar or toolbar.

Sort   A feature that organizes records from A to Z or Z to A, based on one or more fields in a table or query.

Source document   The document from which information will be copied into the clipboard.

Startup window   The window that appears when you start Access; the area from which you carry out database operations.

Status bar   A horizontal bar at the bottom of the screen that displays information about commands or actions and descriptions of ToolTips.

Tab order   Determines the order in which you advance from one field to the next when you press [Tab] to enter data in a form.

Table   A collection of related records in a database.

Table Wizard   A feature that guides you through the process of creating a simple table, prompting you to choose from a variety of fields and options.

Toolbar   A horizontal bar with buttons that provide access to the most commonly used Access commands.

ToolTip   When you move the pointer over a button, the name of the button appears under the pointer and a description of the button appears in the status bar.

Unbound control   A control that is entirely stored in the design of a form or report. There is no link to data in a table. For example, a title above a group of controls is an unbound control.

Wildcards   Symbols that can be used to substitute for characters in text.

Wizard   A feature that provides a series of dialog boxes that guide you through the process of creating a table, form, report, query, or other Access object; unique to Microsoft products.

Index

Special Characters

A

B

C